I0826084

LIBER LIBRORUM.

Liber Librorum:

ITS

STRUCTURE, LIMITATIONS, AND PURPOSE.

A

FRIENDLY COMMUNICATION

TO

A RELUCTANT SCEPTIC.

NEW YORK:
CHARLES SCRIBNER & CO.
1867.

CONTENTS.

NOTES.

PREFACE TO THE AMERICAN EDITION.

The author of Liber Librorum firmly believes and earnestly defends the Historic Reality and the Supernatural Origin of the Mosaic and Christian systems. He also accepts the Incarnation, the Resurrection, and the Redemptive work of Christ, and the other important truths which these involve. In respect to all these points, his position is decisive, and strongly taken against the scepticism which is so fearfully prevalent in both England and America, in the form of an avowed rejection of these facts and truths, and of a secret misgiving that they may perhaps be outgrown, or set aside by the progress of modern thinking.

He insists also upon the supreme authority of the Scriptures in respect to all questions of religious faith, and upon their permanent and indispensable superiority above all other books, as composed by men divinely aided and inspired. But he contends, that to assert for them any higher authority or inspiration, is to claim for them more than they claim for themselves, as well as to take a position that is both untenable and damaging to the interests of Christianity. To explain and vindicate what the author believes to be the correct view of inspiration, is one of the principal objects of this treatise. He has had the sagacity to discern, and the courage to avow, that the question of inspiration must be fairly met, and can no longer be either safely or honestly thrust aside. Dr. Arnold of Rugby wrote in 1835 of "the approaches to that momentous question, which involves in it so great a shock to existing notions; the greatest, probably, that has ever been given since the discovery of the falsehood of the doctrine of the Pope's infallibility. Yet it must come, and will end, in spite of the fears and clamours of the weak and bigoted, in the higher exalting and more sure establishing of Christian truth." The author of LIBER LIBRORUM believes that the time for discussing this question has fully come, and he discusses it like a brave and honest man, by looking squarely in the face the difficulties which attend the traditional theories. He does not, however, write for those whose hereditary faith is as yet undisturbed, but for the 'reluctant sceptics' who find insuperable difficulties in accepting what they conceive to be the current views of Christianity and the Scriptures.

His leading positions may be briefly characterised by those which he opposes and rejects.

1. He opposes the "bibliolatry" which idolizes the letter of the Scriptures as against the claims of the Scriptures themselves, and the spirit of their contents.

2. He opposes the pretensions of High Church arrogance, and the pharisaism of sensuous ritualism.

3. He rejects also the narrowness of that theological dogmatism which reads every term and phrase of its creed and catechism between the lines of the Scriptures, and refuses to revise the traditions of schools of theology by the aid of better methods of interpretation.

It would be idle to expect that all the opinions expressed in a volume written in such a spirit, and with such aims, will or ought to satisfy every reader. Some of these opinions are given as conjectures; others are manifestly not well considered. Some of the views of the writer, in respect to future retribution, will be generally set aside, as unsupported by the testimony of the Scriptures. In respect to some points the work betrays marks of haste, both in thought and composition. But its spirit is earnest, honest, and Christian. It is believed that, as a whole, it is eminently adapted to relieve the difficulties of the "reluctant sceptic," and that it will be welcomed by all those Christian believers who, in these times of trial to their common faith, have full confidence that a frank recognition of the difficulties of their argument is the only wise method of securing for it a triumph. While the book is not, and does not claim to be, an exhaustive argument for the truth of Christianity, it has at least this merit, that it successfully defends it against the ignorance and weakness of many of its defenders.

PREFACE.

Whatever may be the cause, it is but too certain that in the present day, both at home and abroad, multitudes of *religious* young men, who a few years ago would have ranked as believers, are now, instead of attaching themselves to the Church, silently but rapidly becoming alienated from all Christian worship and communion.

'The fact,' says a recent writer, 'may be explained as a passing fashion, or as the result of a certain phase of opinion, but *it is a fact.* And its gravity is heightened by the circumstance that we meet it in men whose lives are pure, who exhibit least of the worldly self-seeking spirit, who are among the most thoughtful and cultivated. The conventional formulæ of the indifference of the corrupt heart or of the love of earthly things are wholly insufficient to explain a state of mind than which none is fraught with greater danger.'

This general unsettlement of religious belief, it is further remarked, has 'grown *from within;* the outcome of it is a scepticism *reluctant* rather than aggressive, which in some of the best men is rapidly passing the border of intellectual hesitation.'

The secret of the success which now attends publications intended to advance a destructive criticism is, that 'they speak to men already 'perplext in faith, but pure in deeds,' who received with their first instruction in Christianity statements of doctrine which, in the time of mature reflection, appear to contradict the Divine instincts of justice, mercy, and truth,—the image of God's own eternity in the heart of man. These doctrines, taught as necessary inferences from, or as identical with the facts of Christianity, were once acquiesced in as the creed of Christendom, but now, in not a few cases, *repulsion* follows the attempt to read and understand them by the light of reason and conscience.'*

That it may be very difficult to render service to such persons without paining or perplexing timid and anxious spirits is but too probable; but everything of a merely personal character ought surely to be risked by Christians on behalf of men and women who, even in their unbelief, have not cast off the reverential feeling for Scripture which they acquired in youth, and who are always willing to allow that to a Bible training they mainly owe the light and life in and by which they now see.

* Contemporary Review, art. 'Indian Questions,' No. 1, p. 125.

The following Correspondence will perhaps serve to explain the state of things to which reference has been made, better than any merely general observations could do.

March 1867.

CORRESPONDENCE.

(I.)

A LETTER.

My dear ——,

Your request that I should lay frankly before you my views regarding the Bible, and that I should state distinctly the particular difficulties which have led me to reject it, is certainly a reasonable one. Yet I can scarcely enter on the subject without pain; nor would I pursue it, did I not feel rather desirous of explaining to you the true position of a multitude of young men who are but too often maligned or misunderstood.

Regarding myself, I need only say that you have known me too long and too well to be in any danger of attributing my unbelief to *moral* perversion. My manner of life, from my youth up, has been no secret to you, and I have consequently little fear that you will so grossly misjudge me as to suppose that I have any wish to escape obligation by cherishing scepticism, or any desire to justify lawlessness by denying Divine Law. But I wish to say a word or two on this point for others.

The unbelievers of the present day, so far, at least, as I have come into contact with them, are not, as you seem to think, irreligious men. They are not mockers, neither do they sit in the seat of the scornful. Hundreds of them are, at the present hour, 'wearying their souls to solve the problem how to conciliate the convictions to which the tendencies of the age have borne them with respect for time-honoured institutions, and tenderness for the faith of those whom they most love and honour.'

You would be surprised to find how many of these have been educated evangelically; how many of them are persons of pure minds, generous, benevolent, and self-denying; how willing many of them are to admit that to the Christian education they have received they owe everything they possess.

It is a mistake to imagine that all, or even the greater part, of these persons either deny the truth of Christianity, or shrink from avowing their conviction that Jesus Christ was the greatest and best being that ever dwelt on earth. They do not dispute that the Bible has, in many respects, a claim to be regarded as the first of books. What they deny is, its Divine character, its authority, its infallibility. They are conscious enough of the darkness which, apart from revelation, hangs over the world in which they live, but they do not see evidence that the Bible has removed that darkness. On the contrary, the more the world advances on its way, and the greater the extent of human knowledge, the deeper seems to them the gloom and mystery which encompasses all things. Life and Death they regard alike as unknown and unknowable. Shadows, in the view of *some*, fall even on the character of God. His very existence is by such at times doubted. Whether, if existent, He is benevolent or malignant, they think cannot be proved. It is *possible*, they say, when in these moods, that God *is*; possible that He is good; possible that after death, life may be renewed; but *nothing is certain.*

To affirm that men who are in this state of mind are unhappy is often, but not always, true; for the mind, like the eye, can accustom itself to darkness as well as to light, and where absolute certainty cannot be obtained, the soul can find rest even in a bare possibility.

Anything, they think, is better than a Gospel, so called, which is in fact no gospel or good news at all, since it consigns all but a fraction of the human race to irremediable sorrow; which exaggerates human sin, and limits Divine mercy; which throws no sunshine on the dark spots that rest upon humanity, and which brings no balm to those that need it most—the slaves of evil, of ignorance, and of superstition.

As a rule, however, they have no wish to undermine the faith of others, and no desire to deprive anyone of consolations which are dear to him. Their spirit is critical, but not contemptuous; it is historic, not intolerant. They disbelieve in miracles, but they have no disposition to laugh at those who hold to them. That which is to believers a question of Life or Death is to them a matter of pure indifference. Where others are enthusiastic, they are calm and judicial.

To these men I adhere. Their number is much greater than you think, and it is constantly increasing. They have their faults without doubt, but in this respect they are only on a par with their opponents. They may sometimes forget what is due to the cherished beliefs of wise and good men who have inherited the opinions of a dead past, but the rudeness is not wanton; it arises from the absence of reverence for what others esteem to be Divine rather from any feeling of animosity. Forgive them this wrong, and believe me when I say that whatever your opinion may be of any of us, our own conviction is that we are doing a good work, that we are striving to establish the principle of freedom of enquiry, in opposition to that of *acquiescence in dogmas* utterly at variance, as we think, not only with the discoveries of science, but with the first principles of morality.

We are ready to avow our belief that the Bible is responsible for the prevalence of the dogmas to which we object, and therefore, 'while we admit the good that is to be found in it, while we neither altogether reject or despise its teachings, we cannot allow it to be held in the estimation that has hitherto been accorded to it, nor can we permit either it or anything else to come between conscience and God.'

We think that the Bishop of Natal has demonstrated that the Sacred Records, as they are called, are not, as a whole, historical, and therefore that the moral and spiritual propositions contained in these books cannot be authoritative. When, therefore, we find in Scripture actions recorded and commended which are immoral; commands given which are iniquitous; and statutes ordained which are unjust; we put them aside just as we should do if they were found in any other book. We maintain that many things in the Bible are untrue, and others morally wrong; among the latter we reckon the Mosaic laws regarding slavery, and the instructions given for the extermination of whole tribes. We are amazed and confounded when we discern that some of these things have been palliated in the writings of a man so great and good as was Dr. Arnold, and that even Lord Macaulay should speak of the Jews as specially selected by God to be 'the ministers of His vengeance, and specially commanded by Him to do many things which, if done without His authority, would have been atrocious crimes.' The principle which underlies this demoralising process is, I need not say, more speciously, and therefore more perniciously, laid down by Bishop Butler in his 'Analogy.'

On the general question of inspiration, my own notion is that it ought not to be regarded as anything peculiar to the past, since we are all, in a certain sense, inspired. All truly great men are unquestionably inspired men. On your own showing, every Christian is inspired who is made a partaker of the Holy Ghost. Do you not recognise this fact when you pray, 'Cleanse the thoughts of our hearts by the inspiration of thy Holy Spirit?' Do you not affirm it when you claim for the godly the promise of the Comforter—'He shall guide you into all truth?' Can you, then, really believe that Biblical inspiration is anything more or less than the combination in the writers of the two fold gift—genius and piety? I myself agree with Mr. F. W. Newman, when he says that only one kind of inspiration can be admitted, namely, that of 'an ordinary influence of the Divine Spirit on the hearts of men, which quickens and strengthens their moral and spiritual powers, and is accessible to all (in a certain stage of development) in some proportion to their own faithfulness.' Of course, this is but intuition, and, holding it, the value and importance of revelation in the Scriptures becomes very small indeed: but I cannot help that.

Professor Strauss somewhat expresses my thought when he says that 'God has revealed Himself to mankind *at all times*—in their own minds, in the works of creation, in the history of the nations, and, finally, in some particularly gifted men whom He raised up as lawgivers and prophets, as teachers and apostles. Such men have risen among all nations, but chiefly amongst the Jews, who very early entertained the notion that there is but one God, that He is the Almighty Creator of heaven and earth, that He is not to be represented by any image or likeness, that He is the Holy Lawgiver, the just Ruler of the destinies of mankind. The religious writings of the ancient Jewish nation being the only ones in which this foundation of true religion is to be found so pure and strong (for which reason even the New Testament relies on and appeals to the Old in this respect) they are also holy to us; and the books of Moses and Samuel, the Psalms, and the Prophets are indispensable to our edification.

'But they are not trustworthy as records of actual facts. Several remarkable events undoubtedly happened to the Israelitish nation, chiefly in the early period of their history; they had escaped from servitude in Egypt under strange circumstances, and after a long migration they had conquered the land of Canaan in bloody wars. These occurrences, of course, continued to live in the mouths of the people from generation to generation. At length some pious Israelite, dwelling on the Divine activity with regard to the departure from Egypt, imagined it in the form in which it stands, *as if* God had ordered Moses in an oral conversation to deliver His people—*as if* He had visibly, in the pillar of cloud and of fire, marched before the army, and so forth. This, written down in after times, is probably the real origin of the relations thereof in those writings that are commonly called the books of Moses.' In this way, that which is recorded in the Old Testament as supernatural may, I think, be accounted for.

So with the New Testament. 'The first Christians naturally asked themselves *whence* in Christ comes this clearness of mind, this sublimity of spirit, this purity of heart which is nowhere else to be found in any human being? He was not produced by sinful seed, *was their answer*; He immediately descended from God, the fountain of all light. This most likely gave rise to the relations of His supernatural production contained in the Gospels of St. Matthew and St. Luke. As a higher spirit *He appeared* to have come down upon this earth for a short time; after His departure from it *He seemed* to have returned to God, whence He came. This again gave rise to the relations of His resurrection and ascension, and so forth.'

'Christ will indeed come back to judge the world; only His coming to judge us is not one that is always delayed from century to century, and never takes place; but the Lord passes judgment every day, for He has given His spirit into our hearts to judge us: punishing us when we are doing or coveting evil, and rewarding us with peace and happiness when we are guided and governed by it. And thus our inward judge—our conscience—purified and sharpened by the Spirit of Christ, is adjudging and preparing to us already in this life reward or punishment, happiness or sorrow, according to what we deserve. This clearly indicates that also in a future life the

Divine Judge will assign to each of us that mansion in His Father's house which he has made himself worthy of here on earth."[1]

I grant that, in one sense, under this mode of treatment, the Book goes, but in another it remains; remains 'to be read more intelligently than ever, not as the infallible Word of God, which it is not, but the fallible word of man, which it is; read as containing a record, not of what God said and did, but of what the best minds in past ages *thought* God said and did. Truth in this way develops. The God of David is an improvement on the God of the book of Joshua. Isaiah's God is not like the God of Moses or of Abraham. The "Father" revealed by Jesus is holier, wiser, and purer than them all. Men will indeed have to give up the superstitions of other days—the dogmas that were accepted on trust—the dreams of dim ages past and gone; but they will build on a surer foundation—they will have a nearer and a dearer faith in One who speaks to His faithful sons *to-day*; and they will build their faith and hope on a better thing than an infallible book (even though they could have it), for they will build on an infallible God, who will give to all who seek Him the witness of His own blessed Spirit that "now are we the sons of God." Then we shall all see plainly that the Bible is our helper and not our master; that it belongs to the experience and the literature of the past; and that while we reverence and study it, we are not to build all our hopes upon it, but that we are to trust to the same God as David and Jesus trusted in, that we may receive *in the same way* and to the same end, the wisdom that made them wise and the inspiration that made them good. The Bible is a book of the past, and it necessarily reflects the errors and the limited experience of the past.'[2]

[1] The opinions of Professor David Strauss, as embodied in his letter to the Burgomaster Hirzell, Professor Orelli, and Professor Hitzig, at Zurich, translated and printed for general circulation as a tract.

[2] 'The Light that Pains,' a tract printed for gratuitous distribution.

But, apart from these views, many enquiries must be made before I can accept the Bible. Take the four Gospels for instance. How am I to know *who* wrote them, or *when* they were written? How am I to ascertain what means of knowledge the writers had, and whether or no they were eye-witnesses of what they record? If they were not, I must be told how they got their information. These, and many similar questions, which you good people never seem to trouble yourselves about, appear to me to be essential and imperatively to require an answer.

Do not, however, suppose, I pray you, that, being in this sceptical condition, I must of necessity be altogether destitute of serious piety. By no means. I can, and do still occasionally, worship both in the Established Church and among Nonconformists. What I agree with I unite in; what I dissent from I leave unnoticed. My tastes lead me to prefer liturgical to free prayer, and I cannot but think that one day we shall have forms for public devotion sufficiently æsthetic to gratify the religious sentiment, without involving dogmas which lead only to dispute. It certainly must be allowed that Christianity, whether in all respects true or not in the shape we have it, is eminently useful, highly consolatory to the poor and dependent, a restraint on many which could be ill spared, and an occasion of constant kindness and benevolent activity.

Further, in the absence of individual conviction, Church authority, if not pressed too far, offers many advantages. Amid the restlessness and discomfort engendered by profitless enquiry, it is a satisfaction, in the absence of anything better, to *admit* the fact that the Church represents the belief of centuries, whether those beliefs be accurate or not; and that confidence in her, whether well grounded or otherwise, at least ensures quiet, by pacifying where it may not satisfy, and by fostering habits the tendency of which must unquestionably be favorable to domestic happiness, to social comfort, and to the interests of law and order among all classes in the commonwealth.

Such is my case. I have been perfectly frank with you in stating it, and I cannot but hope that you will answer me in a similar spirit.

Believe me to be,

Yours cordially,

(II.)

THE REPLY.

My Dear ——,

You do me but justice when you express confidence that I shall not attribute the intellectual wanderings of the son of my dearest friend to *moral* causes. I have no right to do this in any case. It is deeply to be regretted that believers should so often be harsh in their judgments of those who, while honest and respectful in their treatment of Scripture, are unable to arrive at settled convictions regarding its authority. Be assured that the highest faith is not favorable either to bigotry or uncharitableness. Confidence in the Bible, when it arises from supposed triumph in argument, or from a blind and hereditary acceptance of its claim, is, I am quite aware, but too often accompanied by an unloving and self-righteous feeling toward unbelievers; but this fault is rarely found among persons who feel and acknowledge that their joy, in truth, is the result of a *subjective experience* of its value, derived from the source and fountain of all truth. And for obvious reasons. The faith which is subjective carries with it that *sense of certainty* which alone gives repose to the spirit—a repose favorable alike to humility and respect for the consciences of others, and every way out of harmony with either anger or arrogance. Only such a faith is, properly speaking, Divine; for 'the light in which a man can no longer call man "master" is light in which he can no longer desire to be called "master." He who has this faith will rarely venture to say when and how, and to what extent, his brother man is rebellious to light and *guilty* in respect of unbelief; will rarely attempt to decide as to who is leaning to his own understanding, or who receiving the Kingdom of God as a little child.'[1]

And now you must allow me to say that I think you have taken far too favourable a view of *a class* who seem to me anything but models for sincere and serious enquirers. Honest doubt, honestly dealt with, is, I believe, injurious to no one; but doubt encouraged and indulged soon becomes a habit of the mind, and a very unwholesome one too, not unfrequently weakening, and sometimes destroying the very capacity for estimating moral evidence. It is by no means rare to meet with doubters who are so *unreasonable* in relation to their difficulties that, in dealing with them, one is more tempted to question the healthiness of the brain than the integrity of the purpose. It is 'the fool' who says in his heart 'there is no God.'

Some men of this stamp whom I have known were obviously under the influence of an intense and morbid egotism, and others were so completely in bondage to a sense of the ludicrous that they seemed absolutely incapable of dealing with anything *seriously*, which could, by a little perverted ingenuity, be made to look grotesque. Few sceptics, I think, are distinguished by the possession of a robust and well-balanced intellect. I doubt not that *among* these persons are to be found many who may fairly claim to be regarded with the greatest consideration and respect. But this is not the case with all. As among believers are to be seen weak minds as well as strong ones; bad men as well as good men; persons who are able to give a sound reason for the hope that is in them, as well as persons who can give no reason at all: so among unbelievers there are not a few who but too plainly indicate that self-complacency and conceit have had very much to do with their doubts, while others are as clearly the victims of pride and a rebellious will—persons who are ob-

[1] Thoughts on Revelation, with Special Reference to the Present Time. By John McLeod Campbell.

viously destitute of all *reverence*, and perhaps it is not too much to say disbelievers alike in truth and goodness. All this may surely be allowed, without disputing for a moment what you have advanced in favour of your friends.

In relation to your own difficulties, it will only be possible, in a brief letter like this, to glance generally at some considerations which you seem to me to have overlooked.

Your views of inspiration are of course not mine. I certainly regard Biblical inspiration—for I here speak of that only—as something very different from either genius or piety, whether single or combined. I do not think it at all akin to what we sometimes call the inspiration of the poet, of the painter, of the sculptor, or of the musician. I am far, indeed, from disputing that the Giver of every good and perfect gift may justly be regarded as endowing men of genius with all that distinguishes them from their fellows, but when I speak of Holy Scripture as inspired I use the word in a much higher sense than this. I regard that book—so far as it is God-breathed at all—as inspired in such an exceptional way as to remove its revelations altogether out of the rank, even of the highest of merely human compositions.

I admit, indeed, that you would have good ground for maintaining the continuance of inspiration amongst us, if your application of the text quoted was a right one. But it is not so. It is a very serious and mischievous mistake to apply the words, 'He shall guide you into all truth,' to every believer. To do so, *except in a very limited sense*, is, in my judgment, to destroy the broadest distinction that can be pointed out between inspired and uninspired communications. I am always ashamed at the arrogance—however disguised as humility—which is implied when good men say, as many do, 'the Holy Spirit has taught me this or that; God fulfils His promise, and guides me into all truth;' when they ought to say, 'God has revealed in the Bible all truth needful for my salvation from evil, and for my spiritual growth. Just as I come to that book in a right spirit, free from pride and prejudice, from selfishness and sectarianism; not governed by inferior motives, not moved by the desire that such or such an opinion of mine may be confirmed by Scripture, but only anxious to know what the Book says; in other words, just so far as I am purified by the Spirit of God, and my will is brought into harmony with the Divine will, shall I attain wisdom. On the other hand, just in proportion as I come to the written word under the influence of evil, of self-will, of bigotry, or of given theological systems, shall I be liable to delusion and darkness. That which was promised to the Apostles was not, *in the same sense*, promised to me. The Lord led them into all truth, *by direct revelation*, that they might be the instructors of the Church in all ages. The Lord will lead me into all truth, only by the subjection of my will—by giving me instructors of the Church in all ages. The Lord will lead me into all truth, only by the subjection of my will—by giving me a loving, candid, and fearless spirit; by purifying and elevating my moral nature, and by bringing me in this state of mind into heartfelt contact with the revelations of Scripture.'

These are my views; and I wish you to believe that, in holding them, I am anything but insensible to the difficulties which embarrass us, in presenting what may be regarded by men in general as satisfactory proof of many things that we often take for granted, such as miracles, the authorship and authenticity of the four Gospels, the formation of the canon, and much beside. I hope, before long, to lay before you some thoughts by which you will see how these things present themselves to my own mind.

I am, I confess, greatly astonished to find that you should be able, with the amount of natural good sense you possess, to accept Strauss's ideological theory, and to content yourself with the assumption that from some unknown cause or other—for a special revelation is denied—the Jews, although every way inferior in general culture to the surrounding nations, were, even in the very earliest times, immeasurably before others in the knowledge of God; so much so, that the writers of the New Testament properly 'rely upon and appeal' to them in this respect; nay, that we ourselves, with equal propriety, regard some portions at least of Jewish literature as 'holy and indispensable to edification.' We believers say so too, and our reasons for thus judging—whatever they may be worth—are before the world. But what are yours? The books themselves, according to your view, while *professing* to be historical, are really not so; the writers, whoever they might be, are confessedly untrustworthy, for while they broadly and repeatedly assert that such and such things are facts, they, in reality, only imagined them. What these 'pious Israelites' assert to have received directly from God they really invented in order to account for things they could not otherwise explain. When they affirm in the most unmistakeable terms that certain miraculous occurrences took place, such as the presence of the pillar of cloud and the passage of the Red Sea, they only 'imagined the Divine activity,' and wrote *as if* the events had actually transpired; *this*, you say, is the real origin of the relations given in the writings commonly called the Books of Moses. In like manner the narratives of the New Testament are but evolutions of human thought, utterly untrue if presented as facts, yet true as relations of what 'the best minds in past ages *thought* God said and did.'

The theory further supposes that when these early intuitions took shape, and were by somebody or other formed into a book, and ultimately accepted as national annals, the compilers or inventors gained their end by moulding the whole into a history the very reverse of what might reasonably have been expected on the supposition that the object was to present documents likely to be pleasing. For what is this Jewish history as we have it, whether true or false, but a record of early degradation, of continued ingratitude, of perversity, obstinacy, and crime? Of the early judges one (Ehud) is represented as an assassin; another (Abimelech), the son of a concubine, is said to have murdered all his family, and to have been cruel enough on one occasion to have burnt alive about a thousand helpless captives, men and women; a third (Jephthah) in civil strife slays above 40,000 of his countrymen; a fourth (Samson) is but a half-civilized giant; and the state of the country generally is at one period morally degraded to such an extent that one entire tribe—Benjamin—had to be all but extirpated. Again, what an unsatisfactory history is that of Saul! What dark stains rest on David! What a sad ending is that of Solomon! What a catalogue of sins and idolatries defaces the glory of succeeding monarchs! Granting, for the sake of argument, that Ezra and his scribes, instead of finding the records said to have been discovered, invented them, this, at least, follows: that such a history, if not felt to be as *true* as it was humiliating, would certainly have excited popular indignation and been rejected at once.

I am bound, however, to suppose that you really believe the narratives of Scripture to be *inventions*, and that you also believe in their utility and in the piety of the men who set them afloat, for you say you do; but I could not have accepted such a statement on any authority short of your own. For what does it involve? Certainly this—that falsehoods are not only innocent but useful, 'absolutely edifying;' that men may be, at one and the same time, untrustworthy and yet 'pious;' that 'the best minds in past ages' were justified in putting forth what they had only *thought*, as what they had seen and heard; in affirming that their subjective feelings were actual and objective facts. I am quite willing to admit that a supernatural revelation has its difficulties; but were those difficulties ten times greater or more numerous than they are, they would not approach the contradictions which are inseparable from the theory you have adopted. Talk about the *moral* difficulties of the Bible, why they shrink into absolute insignificance when compared with an hypothesis which annihilates all distinction between right and wrong, truth and falsehood, giving, in fact, to falsehood the moral power of truth, to wrong-doing the efficacy of that which is right.

You will perhaps say this is not fair; that it is surely possible for a man to *idealize* honestly, and, more than this, to present ideal thought to himself and to others with all the vividness and force of objective reality, without thereby becoming either a cheat or a charlatan. I admit that such a case is possible, but not in relation to the narratives of Scripture. M. Renan has been attempting this feat very lately, in relation to the Resurrection, and never was there a more signal failure. Facts, as has been well said, 'will not bend to this process.' There never were narratives less ideal or more straightforward in their reality; they might have been purposely framed to *contrast* with professed accounts of visions, and to exclude the possibility of their being confounded with such accounts. The recitals show little care to satisfy our curiosity, or to avoid the appearance of inconsistency in detail; but nothing can be more removed from vagueness and hesitation than their definite, positive statements. It is not criticism, but mere arbitrary license, to say that these facts stand for fancies. The very notion is trifling and incredible. We may disbelieve if we will; but to endeavour to make out that plain assertions are visions, is but to take refuge in the most unlikely of guesses.[1]

There is no fact in history more certain than that Jesus Christ appeared in Judea at the time He is said to have done, that He was crucified, that He was believed by His disciples to have risen from the dead, that 'many professing to have been original witnesses of that event and of the Christian miracles generally, passed their lives in labours, dangers, and sufferings voluntarily undergone in attestation of the accounts which they delivered, and solely in consequence of their belief of the truth of those accounts.'[2] May I not add, and call you and your friends as witnesses, that motives connected with these beliefs have in all ages elevated and ennobled those who

[1] Saturday Review, art. on Renan's Des Apôtres.

[2] Paley's Evidence, motto to cap. ii.–ix.

have received them into their hearts with simplicity and love? The theory of Strauss is absolutely worthless.

And now for your assertion that in the Bible may be found commands which are immoral and iniquitous, such as those which direct the massacre of the Canaanites and sanction cruelty to slaves.

Let us take first the slaughter of the Canaanites. What I have to show, according to you, is that since God *did* command the destruction of these people, He was *right* in doing so. To this, however, I demur. In accepting the Pentateuch as historically true, I am simply bound to show, first, that the assertion of a Divine command to the Israelites *to take possession of Canaan by force*, is inseparable from the rest of the narrative; and then to state the limitations under which, as I imagine, such phrases as 'The Lord said' or 'The Lord spake' ought to be received.

I do not myself think Lord Macaulay's way of putting the matter, although a very common, is a right one. I see no evidence either that the Jews were (except in an indirect and limited sense) 'the ministers of God's vengeance,' or that they had a commission to *extirpate* the nations of Canaan. Least of all can I admit that they were 'specially commanded by God to do many things which, if done without His authority, would have been atrocious crimes.' Right and wrong are not different things in God and man, nor can even the Divine Being rightfully do to-day what He Himself declared to be wrong yesterday, for right is always and eternally right.

The argument that such or such a proceeding appears to us, *when judged by the light of the Gospel*, to be unjust, cruel, or any way wrong, is a very sound one for doubting whether God ever sanctioned it—a powerful reason for demanding good evidence that He did so; but it reaches no further. If it can be satisfactorily shown that God *did really command* this or that thing to be done, we must bow in silence; unless, indeed, we mean, with our limited faculties, and still more limited knowledge, to set ourselves up as wiser or better than our Maker. I cannot, however, admit for a moment that, whether commanded by God or not, the conquest of Canaan by the Israelites was *in itself* an atrocious crime, except on the theory which neither you nor I hold to, that war for purposes of conquest is, *under all circumstances*, criminal.

But the question for our consideration is: Did God, in very deed, command the massacre of the Canaanites? A prior question of course arises, which is this: When God communicates His will to man, does He do it in such a way as not only to render mistake as to the command itself impossible, but also to secure infallibility as to the means employed in its execution?

To neither of these questions can an absolutely affirmative reply be given. Admitting—which we certainly must, if we hold to the Book—that God spake unto Moses, Joshua, and Samuel, *intelligibly*, whether revealing His character, or commanding certain things to be done, we are nevertheless altogether in the dark as to *the mode* in which this was accomplished. We cannot get beyond the Apostolic statement, that the same God who hath 'in these latter days spoken unto us by His Son,' did 'at sundry times and *in divers manners* speak unto the fathers by the prophets' (Heb. i. 1).

But, accepting this statement, what follows? Why clearly this: that as *a true apprehension* of the message of 'the Son' is made dependent on the state of the heart of each individual to whom it comes, so must it be with *every* message God gives or sends to the children of men. Eminently is this the case when the communication relates to anything that has *to be done by man.* Paul had to withstand Peter as a man to be blamed in relation to the particular course he was pursuing in doing God's work. Moses, in fulfilling a Divine command, sinned grievously; nor is there the slightest reason to suppose that any servant of God is, or ever was, free from liability to error in executing the Divine will, if pride or ambition, or selfish passion in any form, mingles with the work. Before, therefore, we 'charge God foolishly' with sanctioning wrong, let us be quite sure that He commanded the thing to be done in the way it was.

The ordinary impression seems to be that a constant and direct intercourse went on between the early rulers of the Jews and their Heavenly King, under which error was impossible; that every act of the government was directed and regulated by intimations from above; that the judges or governors of Israel were but the passive recipients of Divine instructions; that the obedience rendered was therefore, to a great extent, mechanical, leaving little, if any, place for the judgment of the statesman. Something like this is commonly held by persons who, without much reflection, think and speak of the people of Israel as placed under a theocratic government. But such a view of things cannot be sustained from Scripture. On the contrary, there can be no question as to the fact that intimations of the Divine will, as to what the Jews should do under given circumstances, always left room for wisdom or folly in the execution, for judgment or want of judgment in the ruler, for partial or entire obedience in the people.

The distinctions commonly drawn by Christian writers between the old dispensation and the new, generally involve error in the way of exaggerating differences. Lord Bacon asserts broadly that 'Prosperity is the blessing of the old Testament; but that adversity is the blessing of the New.' Archbishop Whately, annotating on this observation, remarks: 'The distinguishing characteristic of the old covenant, of the Mosaic Law, was, that it was enforced by a system of *temporal rewards* and *judgments*, administered according to an extraordinary (miraculous) providence. The Israelites were promised as the reward of obedience, long life, and health, and plentiful harvests, and victory over their enemies. And the punishments threatened for disobedience were pestilence, famine, defeat, and all kinds of temporal calamity. These were the rewards and punishments that formed the *sanction* of the Mosaic law. But the new covenant, the Gospel, held out as its sanction, rewards and punishments in the next world, and these only.'

Facts, however, do not bear out these statements, *except with many limitations.* Asaph was so perplexed by observing the prosperity of the wicked in life, and their tranquillity in death, *contrasting*, as he saw it did, with the frequent misfortunes of the righteous, that he could get no peace until he went into the house of God and meditated on their latter end (at the day of judgment). And, on the other hand, certainly nothing can be more true than your assertion that God is judging us all every day, sometimes rewarding and sometimes inflicting punishment, according to a man's obedience or disobedience.

The truth is, we commonly fall in this matter into a double mistake. We are foolish enough to think that because the action of God is not always obvious to us, He has now *less to do* with the world's affairs than He once had. We *exaggerate* the extent of His interference in former times, because it related more than it does now to the outward and visible. We ought to remember that *at no time* does God manifest Himself more frequently or more directly than is needful, while *at all times* He leaves us to *apply* the principles He has laid down to practical life, as a part of our probation, a course which of necessity involves the possibility of error on our side.

The declaration, 'The Lord said,' 'The Lord spake,' or phrases of similar import, occur probably a hundred times in the Pentateuch alone, and in by far the greater part of these cases the words are used, *not* as asserting in each separate case a direct and immediate Divine revelation, but as implying the settled convictions of the speaker as to the Divine will. They denote in these cases *the application* of Divine statements to given circumstances, by good, but human and therefore fallible, men. Further, we are strangely apt to forget that 'the severity' of God is far more seen in His dealings with the chosen people than with their enemies. In the wilderness, on one occasion, fourteen thousand die of plague, on account of transgression. On another, many perish by the sword. On a third, the earth opens and swallows up offenders. On a fourth, fiery serpents are sent in punishment; while the frightful calamities brought upon Judea by the Romans, to say nothing of the previous overthrow of Jerusalem by the Chaldeans—*all* these events being distinctly put before us as *judicial*—involved miseries quite as great as any that the Canaanites suffered.

In relation to these nations, *the assumption* almost always made is, that God commanded their entire extirpation on account of their crimes. But this is not sustained by the narrative. The *command* is, 'Thou shalt *drive them out* before thee. . . . . Thou shalt make no covenant with them, nor with their gods. They shall not dwell in thy land, lest they make thee sin against Me.' (Exod. xxiii. 32–33.) 'Ye shall destroy their altars, break their images, and cut down their groves: lest thou take of their daughters to thy sons, and go a-whoring after their gods.' (Exod. xxxiv. 11–17.) The *promise*, renewed from time to time, is: 'I will send hornets before thee, which shall drive out the Hivite, the Canaanite, and the Hittite from before thee.' Again: 'I will send an angel before thee; and *I will drive out* the Canaanite.' (Exod. xxxiii. 2.) Further, *as a fact*, 'multitudes of them did flee, some into Africa, and others into Greece. Procopius says they first retreated into Egypt, but gradually advanced into Africa, where they built many cities.'[1] They were never destroyed, except when their evil influence could not in any other way be got rid of.

When the Israelites *fought*, they naturally adopted the ordinary laws of war—the only laws which prevailed in their time—and, in accordance therewith, they slew or made slaves of their enemies. Had the Canaanites been the conquerors, they would, in like manner, have slain or enslaved the Israelites.

[1] Calmet, edited by Taylor.

'But,' you will say, 'the Lord, according to the Bible, *commanded* the slaughter of women and children.' This, however, is not as clear as at first sight it seems to be. The first instance in which this practice occurs is in the case of the Midianites, who had brought such grievous calamities on Israel by seducing the people to idolatry and immorality, *in order that* they might offend God. (Numb. xxv. 1–18 and xxxi. 16.) Here they, in the first instance, slew only the kings of Midian and their warriors. Moses, however, is wroth at this forbearance, and commands the execution of all the male children and of all the women who were not virgins. That the great lawgiver was justified in so doing we have no right to assume. His *motive* was doubtless the preservation of the people, but he does not appear to have had any Divine sanction for this severity. (Numb. xxxi. 14–20.) A little later we have a recital of the general direction to '*drive out*' all the inhabitants, and to '*destroy* all their pictures and images,' but nothing is said about killing the people. (Numb. xxxiii. 52–56.) This direction had, however, been *exceeded* by the Israelites, for when Sihon, king of the Amorites, refused to let them pass, they destroyed all they overcame, even the women and the little ones. In thus acting, they but too plainly imitated the habits of the nations by which they were surrounded.

Once embarked in this ruthless course, they pursued it in the case of Og, king of Bashan, as well as with others. Moses certainly approves this slaughter in his address at Horeb, giving as the reason the prevention of intermarriages, and consequent idolatry. (Deut. vii. 1–11 and xx. 16–18.) Joshua follows the example at Jericho (Josh. vi. 21); at Ai (viii. 25); at Lachish, at Debir, and in other places (x. 40). But it is here to be remarked, that this course is only taken with those tribes who came into battle. It is evident that the Canaanites might have made peace if they would, for it is remarked, 'There was not a city that made peace with the children of Israel, save the inhabitants of Gibeon.'

If Moses, in the address referred to, was infallible—if he was but the mouthpiece of God in the directions he gives to save alive of the seven nations 'nothing that breatheth'—it is clearly not for us to dispute the command; but if, as Dr. Pye Smith has put it, 'the sanction of the New Testament to the inspiration of the Old extends only to 'holy things,' and that 'to attach it to other things is to lose sight of its nature, and to misapply its design,' it is at least an open question whether this was the case. That God was not *pledged*, so to speak, to extirpate the Canaanites, although He supernaturally assisted the Israelites in obtaining possession of the land, is clear from the fact that *the work was not done* wherever it was unnecessary. Miraculous aid, indeed, appears to have been withheld after the primary end—possession of the land—had been attained. We are distinctly told that the children of Israel *could not* drive out the Jebusites. (Josh. xv. 63.) And, again, 'The Lord was with Judah, and he (Judah) drave out the inhabitants of the mountain; but *could not drive out* the inhabitants of the valley, *because they had chariots of iron.*' (Judg. i. 19.) In other cases, when the Israelites became strong enough to conquer, they not only refrained from slaughter, making the people tributary, and dwelling among them, but intermarried, became idolatrous, and forsook the God of their fathers. (Judg. iii. 5–7.) As a consequence of this apostasy, they became themselves, from time to time, slaves: first, to the king of Mesopotamia (iii. 8), then to the Moabites (iii. 14), then to the Canaanites (iv. 2, 3), and then to the Midianites (vi. 1). During all these years, Israel enjoyed the Divine help only at long intervals, and then providentially rather than theocratically, since it was by the raising up of men as deliverers who were sometimes anything but good or godly.

You will perhaps say I have purposely omitted any notice of a case which cannot be explained by the foregoing considerations, viz., that of the Amalekites destroyed by Saul under the directions of Samuel. (1 Sam. xv. 2, 3.) The prophet here certainly claims to speak for God, when he says to Saul, 'Go and smite Amalek, and utterly destroy all that they have, and spare them not; but slay both man and woman, infant and suckling, ox and sheep, camel and ass.' The command appears to have been executed, except in so far as Agag himself was concerned and the cattle. For saving these, Saul is rejected from being king over Israel (xv. 23).

The question arises, Did Samuel, in issuing this command, act by the immediate direction of God, or was the order given under an erroneous impression that in this act of destruction he was but carrying out a Divine threatening, and justifiably accomplishing a great work of retribution? Probably the latter. He believed, doubtless, that he was but uttering the Divine Will when he said, 'Hearken thou unto the voice of the words of the Lord,' and yet it is anything but certain that he was right in thus speaking. He was evidently not infallible or quite free from secondary motives in what he did as the representative of God, or he would not have appointed his sons judges—men 'who turned aside after lucre, and took bribes, and perverted judgment.' (1 Sam. viii. 3.) He was now old, and if he erred in the one instance why should he not in the other? Besides, it is not a little remarkable that while he tells Saul that God had, *on account of this act of disobedience*, rejected him from being king, he had, *before this occurrence*, deposed the son of Kish for offering sacrifice without authority (xiii. 13, 14).

That there was not *the same degree* of personal superintendence, so to speak, on the part of the Divine Being over the Israelites, *after* the making of the golden calf, as there had been before, is evident from the word of the Lord to Moses on that occasion: 'Go, lead the people into the place of which I have spoken unto thee: behold *mine Angel*' (as distinguished from the more immediate presence of God which had hitherto been enjoyed) 'shall go before thee.' (Exod. xxxii. 34.) It has been supposed by some that this was reversed on the intercession of Moses (xxxiii. 12–17), but such does not appear to have been the case. The 'presence' of the Lord with the angel is all that is promised. The probability is, that, step by step, the more immediate interference of God was exchanged for ordinary providential government, as the people gradually assumed the position and responsibilities of an organised nation. If this be true, the likelihood of the command to destroy Amalek being given by Samuel rather than by God is greatly increased.

It is clear enough that none of the judges were 'perfect before God.' Samson's conduct speaks for itself. Gideon kills Zeba and Zalmunna, saying he would have saved them alive if they had not killed his brothers. (Judges viii. 19.) Jephthah and Gideon, Deborah and Barak, in like manner, are seen to act in a spirit and under motives which are far from being unmixed. Samuel, like them, was liable to err; nor does this conclusion at all interfere with the apostolic declaration that 'through faith' these very men 'subdued kingdoms, wrought righteousness, obtained promises, and (figuratively) stopped the mouths of lions.' (Heb. xi. 32.) Great faith is not unfrequently accompanied, especially in warriors, by great defects and grievous deficiencies.

By drawing a distinction, then, between what God clearly commanded, and what men actually did, the difficulty created by the massacre of the Canaanites in great measure vanishes; the Jews cease to be 'ministers of Divine vengeance,' and crimes committed find no excuse in Divine commands. The wickedness of the Canaanites might well justify their expulsion—a wickedness so great and so seductive, that, in order to prevent its spread, 'the Lord went before' both the children of Lot and the children of Esau, driving out the offenders, just as He did before the children of Israel. (Deut. ii. 21, 22.)

And now let us look at the question of slavery. As to its permission at all it must be remembered that neither under the old covenant nor under the new, does God ever appear to do more than establish principles, which, at the proper time, and when men are somewhat prepared for change, are sure to overthrow existing wrongs. Slavery, polygamy, the gladiatorial shows, feudalism, and many other evils, have all in turn fallen by processes which were slow in operation, but sure as to their result. The Israelites, it must be recollected, although a chosen people, had been long slaves in Egypt, and when they came out they were at best but a sort of half savage mob, although wonderfully organized. The legislation both of the wilderness and of the promised land is, in all cases, adapted to the men *as they then were*, and to the world as it existed at that time. The slaughter or the slavery of conquered tribes was the rule everywhere. Tyranny and oppression of the grossest kind was practised by every neighbouring people without restriction or rebuke.

The Israelite alone was under a law which required him to defend the weak, and to carry out with more or less stringency the great principle of love to all men. To what an extent he failed to do this we know too well; but we are in no position whatever fitting us to judge as to the merit or demerit of any enactment intended, not for all time, but for a peculiar people, and for these only at a particular period of their history. All revelation is of necessity *progressive.* It grows with the growth of ages. Wisdom always adapts itself to different times and to different conditions of men. It is only so far as the eye of the mind is opened by experience and discipline that it can take in the truth which is presented to it.

It is easy to seize, as Dr. Colenso has done, upon a single enactment, such as that recorded in Exodus (xxi. 21), where, if, after a severe beating, the slave survived a day or two, the master was to escape punishment, and, *assuming* it to be a Divine Law, to enlarge on the cruelty it seems to sanction; but in so doing some things are taken for granted, and other things are forgotten. First, it by no means follows that because God governed Judea theocratically He is, so to speak, to be made responsible for every enactment found in the laws of Moses. A greater lawgiver than Moses, indeed, never arose; a man more richly endowed with gifts and graces fitting him for the precise work he had to do never lived; but these very gifts prove that he was not a mere passive recipient of Divine instructions. He was left, without doubt, in many matters of detail to judge and act as he saw best for the people he had to govern.

A distinction is clearly drawn between the giving of the ten commandments and the Mosaic Law generally. Regarding the first, it is said, 'the Lord spake unto you out of the midst of the fire.' *He* '*declared* unto you His commandments; and *He wrote* them upon two tables of stone.' Regarding the last, 'The Lord *commanded me* at that time to teach you statutes and judgments.' (Deut. iv. 12–14.)

Why, too, should we shut our eyes to the fact that 'many of the rites prescribed appear to have been taken from those of the Egyptians? The linen garments of the priests, the long hair of the Nazarites, the offering of the first fruits, and similar ordinances, betray an Egyptian origin. All were rejected that savoured of, or countenanced idolatry, or were unsuitable to the national character and state of the Israelites. The wisdom of not introducing new rites and customs is obvious. The people, rude and uncultivated as they were, would have been reluctant to observe strange regulations. They adhered with pertinacity to what they had learned and seen. Hence we perceive the propriety of retaining as many old ordinances and ceremonies as were adapted to the purpose which God had in view by giving the Levitical law."[1]

Further, it should be borne in mind that, by the very same law that is pronounced so cruel, it was provided that if the slave died under his master's hand the blood of the man should surely be avenged. This was a provision which would tend

[1] Davidson's Text of the Old Testament Considered, second ed. pp. 582-3.

powerfully to check any rigour which was accompanied by such a risk. As a fact, the Hebrew slave, whether reduced to this condition by criminality, or bought with money of the stranger, was incalculably better cared for than he would have been among any other people. If a Hebrew, his servitude terminated at the end of six years. (Exod. xxi. 2.) His master was admonished to treat him while in bondage 'as an hired servant,' and 'not to rule over him with rigour.' (Lev. xxv. 39–43.) War captives, such as the Canaanites or others, as well as those purchased from foreign dealers, were protected by statutes unknown elsewhere. The loss of an eye or a tooth was to be recompensed by giving the slave his liberty (Exod. xxi. 26, 27), and his wilful murder entailed the same punishment as in the case of a free man. (Lev. xxiv. 17–22.)

On the whole, it can scarcely be disputed that slavery, as Mr. Bevan suggests in his article in Smith's Dictionary, was in the Mosaic law recognised mainly 'with a view to *mitigate* its hardships. In that phase of society which prevailed when these laws were made,' he remarks, 'slavery was commonly the alternative of death in the case of all who were captured in battle. A labouring class, in our sense of the word, was almost unknown to the nations of antiquity; hired service was regarded as incompatible with freedom; the slave, as a rule, occupied the same social position as the servant or labourer of modern times, though differing from him in regard to political status.' There is nothing whatever in the Mosaic laws relating to slavery, when candidly and comprehensively considered, which in the slightest degree justifies doubt as to the Pentateuch being what it professes to be—a true delineation of God's dealings with His ancient people.

And now let us pass on to other subjects. As I have already observed, I perfectly agree with you when you say that the Lord judges us every day; but I am quite at a loss to understand on what ground you can affirm that Christ '*will come back* to judge the world,' since you neither believe that

God has appointed a day (a fixed time) for that purpose, or that He who is to be the judge of men has been raised from the dead. Denying the resurrection of Christ as an objective fact, how can you hold that He will come back? Refusing to accept what the Bible says as to the beginning of the world, and rejecting also what it affirms regarding the end of it, it is plain that in your view 'all things continue as they were from the beginning of the creation' (2 Pet. iii. 4, 5), and, for anything you know to the contrary, will so continue for ever. A comforting thought, truly, to anyone who contemplates the sin and misery, the oppression and wrong, of which earth is the theatre, and a thought which is certainly not much alleviated by the possibility of improvement through material agencies; for hitherto 'progress' has brought with it almost as many sorrows as joys, by no means *perceptibly increasing* the sum of human happiness. Ah! my dear friend, hide it as you may, unbelief is but another word for darkness and despair.

You continue to speak, I perceive, of the 'witness of the Spirit,' and about being a 'son of God;' but how you can use such terms, or arrive at any assurance that your faith and hope, such as they are, rest on a good foundation, while abandoning Scripture, I am at a loss to imagine; for apart from the Divine revelation which you reject, no ray of light falls upon our path. You may tell me that a blind man has, *by intuition*, the same image on his eye of hill and dale, tree and flower, sun and stars, that I have, but I cannot believe you. I should insist that such a person must have *once* seen, or that *if not recollections*, his supposed intuitions were but conceptions originating in the descriptions of others. So, until I find a man brought up in the darkness of heathenism and altogether unacquainted with Scripture, possessing by immediate revelation from God a sense of sonship, a witness of the Spirit, and a faith and hope akin thereto, I must decline to admit that the case you have put is other than a mere imagination. 'To affirm that each man at once, by internal illumination alone, attains a clear recognition of even elementary moral and spiritual truth, is to ignore the laws according to which the soul's activity is developed, and to contradict universal experience, which tells us that the great majority of mankind are but in partial possession of this spiritual and moral truth, and hold it, for the most part, in connection with the most prodigious and pernicious errors."[1]

I must here, however, allow that you are to some extent right in saying that the Gospel, as ordinarily preached, exaggerates human sin and limits Divine mercy. It exaggerates evil however, only in so far as it abandons the record; only in so far as it *equalises* transgression of all kinds, by measuring the guilt of sin, *not as God does*, by the circumstances under which it is committed—such as the ignorance or weakness of the sinner—but by the glory of the Creator, and the dignity of the Divine Redeemer. It limits mercy only in so far as it makes—without any Scriptural authority for so doing—the *possibility* of pardon to depend on conditions which can only be fulfilled by the comparatively few who *here* become acquainted with the Gospel; only in so far as it teaches that the redeeming love of the Saviour cannot be of any practical benefit except to the elect. The Bible is surely not responsible for these or any other perversions, nor must the *inferences* of man be confounded with the revelations of God.

My letter is unduly lengthening, but I cannot leave entirely unnoticed your expectation—shall I not say hope?—that one day we shall have 'forms of public devotion sufficiently æsthetic to gratify the religious sentiment, without involving dogmas that lead only to dispute.' You will perhaps be surprised if I tell you that I think this very possible. But, believe me, it will only be when Christendom, so long apostate, has, in retribution for her abominations, become absolutely atheistic.

That a tendency of this kind manifests itself, from time to time, in Rome, especially among the Jesuits, has been noticed

[1] The Eclipse of Faith: a Visit to a Religious Sceptic, p. 297.

by devout Catholics, and is regarded by them with grief and anxiety. 'It is well known,' says a Catholic writer (probably belonging to the Eastern branch), 'that the Jesuits assisted, or rather guided the Pope, in bringing out the last dogma of the immaculate conception of Mary. They acted with foresight, since they exalted the *external* veneration of the blessed Virgin, which latter rests on Mary's justification and sanctification through the redeeming merits of Christ—and they were thus enabled to help on still further *the externalising of Christianity*. Externalism is superficiality; superficiality is frivolity; frivolity means *manageableness* by a strong spirit and will.'[1] What England has chiefly to dread in the present advancing love of ritualism is *the scepticism it hides* and the frivolity it engenders and encourages; each, in its own way, fatal to the civil liberty which arises out of religious individuality and its accompaniment—a claim that the supremacy of conscience shall be acknowledged.

The mediæval follies of Rome will not always be endured; but her æsthetic worship, her ritualism, the 'pillows' she has in store for all doubters, the responsibilities she is willing to assume, the charm of her ideal unity, her blandishments, and pomp, and pride will last; and when these are separated—which they easily may be—from any particular form of despotism; when the Christian element, *in her identical with the mediæval*, is eliminated for ever; when the true piety that is in her departs; and when she becomes, as she then will, the embodiment of the spirit of the time—her priesthood intellectual, her splendour unexampled, and mankind everywhere drunk with the wine of her fornication; then, I say, will her mysterious influence survive change, and instead of being weakened, will rule the world with greater power than ever.

Of her intolerance, *for she will retain that*, I say nothing; on the predictions which shadow forth her ultimate ruin, I am here silent; but I cannot help calling your attention to the

[1] Overbeck on Catholic Orthodoxy.

point where scepticism and ritualism meet; where popery and infidelity fraternize, and will one day embrace each other. Beware, I entreat you, of that ending.

The fault that saps the life
Is doubt half crushed, half veiled; the lip assent
Which finds no echo in the heart of hearts.

Far better is it to be restless, even to unhappiness, than to be drugged. Far better is it to be an honest unbeliever than an hypocritical worshipper; for how can any worship be other than simulated which disregards truth, the only pabulum of the soul; which, proceeding on the assumption that God cannot be known, finds in forms and ceremonies a place indeed for a sensuous fancy, but none for the best affections of the soul; which substitutes the sentimental for the heartfelt, and which, in so doing, turns away man's noblest faculty—the imagination, 'the chief connective link between the visible world and the invisible—from its appointed task of spiritualising the senses, to perform the ignoble drudgery of sensualising the spirit.'[1]

One word more, and I have done. I do not dispute what you say as to the *utility* of the Christian religion, whether true or false; but I most firmly hold that we are not taught in Scripture that faith in Christ is intended to be chiefly utilitarian, or that it is a system revealed for the improvement of the present world. The voice of God is, 'Behold, I make all things new.' Only as it finally accomplishes the reconstitution of humanity in a state of purity and blessedness will the purpose of God in its introduction be fully and for ever answered.

Some points to which you have referred I have still left untouched, but I hope before long to be able to resume the subject.

Believe me to be,
Yours very truly,
———.

The following chapters may be regarded as having arisen out of the foregoing correspondence.

[1] Archdeacon Hare's Mission of the Comforter.

LIBER LIBRORUM.

CHAPTER I.

REVELATION AND INSPIRATION.

Most of us, in this country at least, profess to believe in a Divine revelation embodied in an inspired book. We may therefore perhaps, for our present purpose, be allowed to *assume* not only that the Father of our spirits can, if He will, communicate with the creatures He has made, but that He actually has done so through the agency of man; and, further, that these communications, whatever may be their value or extent, are included in the book we call the Bible.

The point for consideration is, What is meant by this assumption? What do we understand by Revelation, and what by Inspiration? Is the book supposed to be inspired *infallible* in its utterances? If so, does this infallibility extend to everything which is therein included? If not, how is the inspired to be distinguished from the uninspired, the human from the Divine? These are the questions which, in one form or other, continually present themselves for solution, and which the men of this generation find themselves obliged to examine afresh, and, if possible, to settle.

Such topics cannot, however, be disposed of lightly or in few words, for they involve matters which must be searched out honestly and without reserve, whether the result be sadness or satisfaction. They are not mere abstract enquiries. The Bible *exists*, and the very fact of its existence, to say nothing of its history, renders it imperative that its pretensions should be either sustained or overthrown. The highest minds that have ever appeared upon earth have reverently bowed before its teachings, and the humblest have been upheld by its consolations. If all alike have been deluded, the delusion is certainly the most remarkable that has ever occurred in the history of our race.

Further, the Book must be treated by itself, and apart altogether from any deductions that have been drawn from its contents; for nothing can be clearer than that Scripture is self-sustained and self-interpreting.

The Sacred Writings contain 'a record of facts, and make an immediate application of the facts, but they do no more; *life* and not thought is the object to which they primarily minister, and so they minister (as no other writings ever could do) to thought *through life*. They set forth a truth with simple distinctness, but do not say *how* it is, or *why* it is.'[1] They are therefore absolutely independent of all commentators, and must not be mixed up with any inferences, or set of inferences, deduced by theologians; with any series of propositions, true or false; with any system of doctrine, however

[1] Westcott on the Resurrection.

apparently conclusive, which may at any time have been framed from the record.

Nor should the Bible be regarded as the *only* channel through which God speaks to man.

Nature is a revelation. 'The heavens declare the glory of God, and the firmament showeth His handywork.' Men are justly blameable who fail to discern God, more or less, in His works. 'For the invisible things of Him, from the creation of the world are clearly seen (being understood by the things that are made), even His eternal power and Godhead.' The guilt of Paganism, whether ancient or modern, is to be measured by the extent to which every individual, in his love of idolatry and its abominations, turns a deaf ear to the teachings of the natural world regarding the one God. The apostle Paul asserts this when he argues that blindness and perversity *shut up* the heathen in sin, and necessitate a Redeemer; although he nowhere says, as many persons affirm, that, remaining what they are during life, they are *shut out* of the Divine compassion. This conclusion, however common, is but a fallible, and probably very inaccurate, human inference.

Family life, again, is a revelation. The ordinance of parent and child reveals God as the Father of spirits. Our Lord recognizes this when He says, 'If ye, being evil, know how to give good gifts unto your children, how much more shall your heavenly Father give the Holy Spirit to them that ask Him.'

The Bible is pre-eminently such only in so far as it makes God known to us; only in so far as it unveils the Divine character, or discloses Divine designs; only in so far as it casts light on what would otherwise be kept from us, because unattainable by the human mind apart from this method of communication.

The precise extent of its teaching; the value of the information it imparts; the limits within which the Book may be regarded as infallible; and the process by which what is Divine in it may be separated from that which is human, will come under our notice in due time. That it *has* a human aspect no one attempts to deny; that it *reveals* chiefly 'through the relations of ordinary daily life;' that it comes to us 'sometimes intermingled with the private histories and varying fortunes of an Eastern people,' is as certain as that it was given 'at sundry times and in divers manners;' but the Book is not on these accounts the less a revelation, nor is it, as a consequence, in any degree unadapted either to our nature or necessities.

INSPIRATION is that process by which God, *for an end*, not only communicates to certain men facts or truths, the knowledge of which could not be attained in any other way; but also the ability to teach to others, without error or defect, the truths thus revealed. Inspiration, therefore, properly so called, implies both reception and utterance, the capacity to receive, and the power to communicate Divine truth authoritatively and infallibly. That which is not infallibly true cannot be a revelation from God. That which is not communicated to man without any admixture of error cannot, properly speaking, be the word of the Heavenly Father.

By an inspired MAN, then, we understand one who has received, by a direct inbreathing of light and truth from God, *a message to others;* a commission involving an obligation, sometimes to speak, sometimes to write, sometimes, under providential guidance, to record faithfully, although not always without liability to error, a fact, or conversation, or discourse; sometimes, under like conditions, to narrate a history; sometimes to compile and edit existing documents; sometimes, by direct inspiration, to write letters; and sometimes to predict future events.

In the execution of such tasks, *infallibility* will doubtless belong to all that has been directly revealed from above; to all prediction founded thereupon, and to all that is communicated by special command; but not by any means of necessity to everything that has thus providentially been preserved from oblivion.

The person so commissioned may thoroughly comprehend his own words, or he may have the depth of meaning involved in his utterances concealed from him. He may, like Luke, write only because 'many having taken in hand to set forth in order a declaration of things surely believed,' it 'seemed good,' to him to write also; or, like Daniel, he may record words respecting which he is obliged to say, 'I heard, but I understood not.' He may, like Paul on one occasion, feel that he speaks 'by permission,' and not by commandment; or, like the same apostle at another time, he may claim to express himself 'not in the words which man's wisdom teacheth, but which the Holy Ghost teacheth.' He may speak with authority, and demand audience as a messenger of God; or he may beseech and entreat, as a fellow-sufferer, that his words may be received with a loving heart, since love alone moves him to utter them. He may be altogether unconscious that he is writing for all time, foreseeing the wants of all generations, and supplying the Church with spiritual nourishment for two thousand years; or he may have some slight and dim intimation that this is the case.

Let these things, however, be as they may, it is indisputable that, if inspired in this high sense, the man is gifted with all that is requisite to enable him to execute the Divine commission faithfully; which he can of course only do by receiving from Him who gave it such *light* as may be needful to enlighten others—such *supernatural guidance* as may be required to preserve him from important error. So far as the apostles were concerned, this sort of help seems to have been directly promised to them by the Saviour, when, speaking of 'the Comforter' that was to come, He says, 'He shall guide you into all truth. He shall *bring all things to your remembrance* whatsoever I have spoken unto you.'

The *way* in which this may be accomplished is no concern of ours. To what extent such men unite with the Divine revealer; how far they themselves accurately understand that which they communicate to others; or how far they are merely passive instruments in the hands of God, it is impossible for us to know, nor is it of any moment that we should have an opinion on the subject. What we want to ascertain is, not *how* apostles or prophets received that which they have recorded, but whether that which they say is their own or God's? whether it is merely a human judgment, or a Divine and therefore authoritative message?

A Book is inspired, just to the extent that it contains knowledge which has been supernaturally communicated *for ends* which could not otherwise have been attained. If, as in the case of the Bible, the communication has been made to men who lived ages ago, the book, or rather those portions of it which embody the divine revelation, is authoritative and unquestionable only to the extent that the original text has been preserved and faithfully translated.

If it can be shown that the series of tracts which constitute the Bible—written, as it is admitted they have been, by men living at different and far distant periods —have, each and all of them, from first to last been thus produced and preserved, *then*, as Mr. Burgon asserts,[1] 'every chapter, every verse, every word, every syllable of it' may be regarded as 'the direct utterance of the Most High,' but not otherwise. Dr. Carson, reviewing a volume on the evidences by the late Daniel Wilson, Bishop of Calcutta, takes this ground and says, 'It requires as much inspiration to tell what o'clock it is by inspiration, as to reveal the Gospel itself.' If all Scripture, he adds, is given by inspiration, 'the reference to Paul's cloak requires as much inspiration as those passages that declare the way of salvation.'

This, however, is mere folly, since Paul obviously neither needed nor enjoyed any help from above, either in expressing his wish that the parchments should be sent, or in any other matter relating to his personal wants or wishes. We may be well assured 'the Divine Being does not resort to miracle *without occasion or beyond occasion*.'

All this may freely be allowed without at all shaking

[1] Inspiration and Interpretation: seven Sermons before the University of Oxford. By the Rev. J. W. Burgon, M. A., Fellow of Oriel College. So, in effect, Gaussen, Haldane, Dr. Candlish, and others.

the foundation on which we rest the assertion, that the Bible is inspired in a sense exceptional enough to remove it out of the rank of even the highest of merely human compositions. For if its teachings be only the words of men so purified and morally elevated that their instructions are weightier, more Godlike, more profitable than those of other men; if they who speak or write have not received that which they tell us is from God, *as a message to be delivered*, they have not been inspired at all, in the only sense which ought to be attached to that word when we connect it with Holy Scripture.

It has already been said that we have nothing whatever to do with *the mode* in which inspired men may be supposed to have received the Divine gift. Perhaps we have as little concern with *the precise form* in which they embody the thought that has been given them; whether it be in prose or poetry, in narrative or in epistle, in parable or in lengthened discourse. All that we want to be assured of is, that certain teaching may reasonably be confided in as Divine, and therefore infallible—that it is, in short, pure truth, without error or alloy. If this assurance cannot be had, it is but folly to attach the importance to the Bible we do, or to seek guidance of men who lived and died eighteen hundred years ago, rather than in the highest spiritual intuitions of our own souls.

The great question then arises, whether the Divine authority claimed in the Bible for prophets and apostles should be extended to all that is recorded in Scripture; whether we ought to affirm of 'the Book' that it is from first to last, and in all parts, 'the Word of God;' or whether we should be content with the assertion that it contains and embodies that Word. If the former view be correct, it is infallible throughout. If the latter, its infallibility must be limited to certain portions. We shall find the enquiry both interesting and important. Let us not be afraid of it.

For the present, it is *assumed* that inspiration, and therefore infallibility, does not belong to the entire book; and, further, that a principle may be found by the application of which that which is inspired may be distinguished from that which is not.

CHAPTER II.

THE EXTENT OF THE CLAIM.

WE have now to enquire what, in relation to its inspiration, the Bible says of itself. Does it, or does it not, affirm that everything contained in the volume as it stands is inspired, and therefore infallible?

The first passage that will probably suggest itself in this connection to most persons, is found in St. Paul's second epistle to Timothy (iii. 16, 17): 'All Scripture is given by inspiration of God, and is profitable for doctrine, for reproof, for correction, for instruction in righteousness: that the man of God may be perfect, throughly furnished unto all good works.' So the words stand in our authorized version, and the text, as is well known, is often claimed as positively asserting that *everything* contained, whether in the Old Testament or in the New, is inspired of God.

But does the writer affirm this? Clearly, not at all; for at the time Paul wrote, no such book as the New Testament was in existence. He could therefore only refer to the Old. Further, the words of the apostle as given in our version are not the words he used. Paul does not say that *all* Scripture (whatever may be included under that designation) is given by inspiration or 'God-breathed,' but that *all Divinely inspired Scripture*—all Scripture, that is, from God—is also profitable. (See Alford, Ellicott, Adam Clarke, and Pye Smith.)

The apostle had, in the preceding verse, been telling his 'son Timothy' that the Holy Scriptures, with which he had been acquainted from his childhood, were able to make him wise unto salvation through faith in Christ, and he now adds, 'All Scripture given by inspiration of God is profitable *for the perfection of character.*' To suppose that he here means to affirm that the catalogue of the Dukes of Edom, given us in the first book of Chronicles, are to be placed side by side with the prophecies of Isaiah or the utterances of the Psalms, that *both* are 'God-breathed' and alike given 'that the man of God may be perfect,' surely savours far more of superstition than of piety.

Nor is this all. For the supposition that the apostle intended to say that all Scripture (meaning thereby all that was then embodied in the Septuagint, *from which he habitually quotes*) was given by inspiration of God, is to make him assert the inspiration of the Apocrypha, for there is every reason to suppose that some at least of the books now known as apocryphal were, even in his day, included in the Old Testament Scriptures.[1] It

[1] The books thus found in the Septuagint version were not, indeed, in the Hebrew text, nor in the canon acknowledged by the Jews of Palestine; but 'they were recognised by the Hellenistic Jews, and, therefore, by the men with whom Paul came more immediately into contact.' In Clement of Alexandria, in Origen and Athanasius, we find citations from the books of the present Apocrypha as 'Scripture,' 'Divine Scripture,' and 'Prophecy.' Augustine admitted several apocryphal books. It was reserved for the age of the Reformation to stamp the word 'apocrypha' with its

is generally supposed that these books obtained a place in the Greek Scriptures about one hundred and thirty years before Christ. 'The only copies of the Scriptures in existence for the first three hundred years after Christ, either among the Jews or Christians of Greece, Italy, or Africa, contained these books without any mark of distinction that we know of. Origen, at great length, vindicates these parts of the Greek version, asserting that they were true and genuine, and made use of in Greek among all the churches of the Gentiles, and that we should not attend to the fraudulent comments of the Jews, but take that only for true, in the Holy Scriptures, which the seventy had translated, for that this only was confirmed by apostolic authority.'[1] The absence of any list of inspired books in the writings of the apostle, and the fact that he commonly quotes from the Greek Septuagint without remark, certainly favours the opinion that St. Paul did not intend to say that *every writing* then regarded as Scripture was inspired.

Other statements made by Paul, by his brother apostles, and by Christ Himself, confirm us in the propriety

present signification. (Rev. E. H. Plumptre, in Smith's Dictionary, art. 'Apocrypha.')

'The absolute infallibility of the sacred books *throughout* was set up by Protestantism as a counterpoise to the infallible authority asserted and claimed by the Romish Church. Protestantism sought to recover, *by means of the outwardly authoritative and entire infallibility of books*, what it had lost by rejecting inspired councils and popish infallibility.' (Tholuck, quoted in Davidson's Introduction, p. 372.)

[1] Kitto's Bib. Cycl. by Dr. Alexander; art. 'Apocrypha,' by Dr. Wright.

of limiting infallibility to portions of the Bible. The following may be quoted: '*Prophecy* came not in old time by the will of man; but holy men of God spake as they were moved by the Holy Ghost' (2 Peter i. 21). 'God who in sundry times and divers manners spake in time past unto the fathers *by the prophets*' (Heb. i. 1). Paul speaks of the faith of the Ephesians as 'built on the foundation of *the apostles and prophets*' (Eph. ii. 20). It may not, indeed, be argued from these passages that inspiration is to be confined to the writings of the prophets; but it is surely worth notice, that in Scripture *prophecy is specially marked out* as given by inspiration. Attach to the word 'prophecy' the meaning it always has in the Bible, viz., not that of prediction merely, but all Divine utterances, and it is found to be only another phrase for 'the oracles of God' (Romans iii. 2); for the 'lively oracles' (Acts vii. 38); for the holy writings (γραφαῖς ἁγίαις) (Romans i. 2); for the sacred letters (τὰ ἱερὰ γράμματα) (2 Tim. iii. 15); and for 'every word that proceedeth out of the mouth of God' (Matt. iv. 4).

That Holy Scripture is not unfrequently *limited* by Christ Himself seems clear. He sometimes speaks of it as if it were confined to 'Moses and the prophets' (Luke xvi. 29–31)—that is, to the revealed law of God whether given by Moses or by later inspired teachers. After the resurrection, we find Him expounding as Divine 'all things written *in the law of Moses*, and *in the prophets*, and in the Psalms *concerning Himself*' (Luke xxiv. 44); but in no part of the Lord's teaching can there be found a word to justify the assertion that everything contained in the Old Testament from

Genesis to Malachi ought to be regarded as equally authoritative and infallible.

It has, indeed, been maintained that in the words just quoted Christ refers to the three great divisions under which, it is supposed, the Old Testament writings were then classed. But there is no evidence whatever of this. To speak of the law of Moses, of the prophets, and of the Psalms, as containing predictions regarding Himself, is surely a very different thing from asserting that the law, the prophecies, and the remainder of the books are integral sections of a completed whole. As reasonable would it be to affirm that Paul taught this triple division of a complete volume, when he tells us that he persuaded the Jews 'concerning Jesus, both out of the law of Moses and out of the prophets.' The triple division is indeed 'very ancient; but it is difficult to say what were included under each of these heads. There was no fixed and unalterable arrangement of the sacred books as that which is commonly assumed anterior to the fifth century of the Christian era.'[1] To rest a claim for the inspiration of the entire volume on such a basis as this, is weakness indeed. Equally unwise is it to conclude, without any good reason for so doing, that every book must be inspired from which Christ or His apostles quoted, especially when it is remembered that non-quotation from any book of Scripture is never regarded as fatal to its authority, and while other books referred to, like that of 'Enoch,' are now unknown. Such passages as 'Thou hast magnified Thy word above all Thy name' evidently do not refer to the Bible as a book.

[1] Kitto's Bib. Cycl., art. 'Canon,' by Dr. Alexander.

Specific assertions of inspiration are indeed not unfrequently put forth; *but none of these apply to the whole volume.* The following may be cited:—

1. There is a claim on behalf of the Divine character of the Mosaic tabernacle services, in the words, '*The Holy Ghost this signifying*' (Heb. ix. 8). Also a very distinct one on behalf of the *direct communications* made to Moses by God: 'Have ye not read that which was *spoken unto you by God*' (Matt. xxii. 31 referring to Exod. iii. 6).

2. For the inspiration of the prophets who spake beforehand of Christ: 'Searching what or what manner of time *the Spirit of Christ which was in them* did signify' (1 Pet. i. 11). And again: 'Prophecy came not in old time by the will of man: but holy men of God spake *as they were moved by the Holy Ghost*' (2 Pet. i. 21). And again: 'Those things which *God before had showed* by the mouth of all His prophets' (Acts iii. 18).

3. For David: 'Which *the Holy Ghost by the mouth of David* spake' (Acts i. 16; iv. 25). For Isaiah: 'Well *spake the Holy Ghost* by Esaias the prophet' (Acts xxviii. 25). For Jeremiah: 'Whereof *the Holy Ghost said*' (Heb. x. 15).

4. Under given circumstances for the apostles generally: 'It is not ye that speak, but *the Holy Ghost*' (Mark xiii. 11.) Paul makes it for himself, when he commends the Thessalonians for receiving his teaching not as his, but 'as it is in truth *the Word of God*' (1 Thess. ii. 13). Elsewhere he says, 'We speak not in the words which man's wisdom teacheth, but which *the Holy Ghost* teacheth' (1 Cor. ii. 13). John, in the

Apocalypse, distinctly affirms that what he reveals was 'sent and signified' to him by Christ (Rev. i. 1).

It is not of course pretended that only those writers are inspired for whom this special claim is made; but it is surely singular that while inspiration is affirmed *generally* of prophets and apostles, and *specially* of some, it is nowhere claimed either generally or specially for historians, or for the entire volume of Scripture. Everything, indeed, indicates that the claim of inspiration, and therefore of infallibility, is limited to those portions of the Bible which are revelations from heaven, or essential to their comprehension.

Under the head, then, of inspired Scripture may be classed all that we are told of God *beyond* what may be gathered from His Works and Providential government of the world; all the information we have as to our future destiny; every prophetic intimation; every elevating and purifying truth which man could not otherwise reach. From it may be excluded without irreverence the merely historical, *however true and useful*; genealogies however important in their place; poems or proverbs *however wise*, which are but expressions of human experience; references to physical phenomena ordinarily expressed in colloquial language; and all acts or utterances which are not in accordance with the spirit and temper of the Lord Jesus. *There are such* in the Old Testament; and as these, however needful to a true delineation of men and times, are not in themselves intended for our imitation, and have no tendency 'to make the man of God perfect,' it is not presumptuous to say that, whatever may be their value, they are but records of human infirmity. Nor is it any answer to reply that from all these portions a devout mind can gain instruction, for by such a mind 'sermons' may be found 'in stones;' but this does not make the stones inspired.

The distinction is not a novel one; it has been urged by some of the ablest and best divines the Church has produced.[1]

We have said that inspiration, whether verbal or otherwise, implies the power of *communicating* the message received from God without error or mistake; it may also be understood to include *the ability* to narrate exactly as they happened all occurrences and conversations *in which absolute accuracy was requisite*, and to select, without failure of judgment, such written memorials as it seemed good to Divine Providence to perpetuate for the use of the Church. But it by no means follows that two inspired men must therefore necessarily narrate events in the same words, or precisely in the same order; nor does such aid either involve the Divine sanction of every act thus recorded, or give a character of Divine truthfulness to every history and genealogy that may be inserted. Further, where communications such as those embodied in the Bible, have been recorded by men who lived ages ago, we must have some evidence that the books containing them have been carefully preserved. This we certainly have.

The preservation of the Old Testament by the Jew —considering what it contains — through thousands of years, obviously implies a Providential care of it,

[1] See Appendix, Note A. 'Eminent Witnesses.'

scarcely less Divine than that which originally attended its formation. Accuracy in translation being within the reach of human industry, has, for that reason, been left to be secured by the unaided energies of man.

And this leads us to the consideration of *certain facts* relating to the Bible, which plainly come under our cognizance, and which certainly *make against* the supposition that everything in the book is Divinely inspired, and therefore infallible, since they show that the Bible has not been preserved from the accidents which are inseparable from the transmission of ancient documents through the ages. On the contrary, it is certain that while, as a whole, the book has been remarkably cared for, it contains, in matters comparatively unimportant, not a few errors and some positive contradictions. These can only be accounted for on one of two suppositions: either that the writers were not in these particulars Divinely inspired and so preserved from the possibility of error, or that the Book itself has, at a later period, been exposed sometimes to wilful interpolation, and sometimes to clerkly inaccuracy.

We take no notice here of alleged contradictions between prophecies and their fulfilment, or of apparent discrepancies in doctrine; for these, whether real or unreal—and we think them, for the most part, unreal—would lead us on to debateable ground. We wish simply to deal with facts which no one can dispute; and therefore only bring forward inaccuracies that are obvious at a glance. The following instances will suffice to show what is meant.

'In the twenty-second chapter of the second book of Chronicles "forty-two years" ought to be twenty-two.

This is evident when the passage is compared with the second book of Kings (viii. 26). Again, in the second book of Samuel (viii. 4), David is said to have taken from Hadadezer "seven hundred horsemen." In the first of Chronicles (xviii. 4) the number is said to have been "seven *thousand* horsemen." In the book of Numbers, "those that died in the plague" (on account of Baal Peor) are said to have been "twenty and four thousand," while in the first of Corinthians (x. 8) it is said, in relation to the same event, there fell in one day *three* and twenty thousand.'

With regard to the numbering of the people mistakes are numerous. E. g.: According to Samuel (2 Sam. xxiv. 9), Joab's report to David after the census is 'eight hundred thousand' fighting men of Israel, and 'five hundred thousand' of Judah. In the first of Chronicles (xxi. 5) the same report is said to have been '*eleven* hundred thousand' of Israel, and 'four hundred and seventy thousand' of Judah. In the first of Kings (xv. 5) we are told that David (as monarch) never deviated from the right 'save in the matter of Uriah the Hittite,' yet we know that he sinned in numbering the people, and was punished for it. Further, in relation to this very punishment, it is said in the second of Samuel (xxiv. 13) that the prophet Gad came to David and said to him, 'Shall seven years of famine come unto thee in thy land?' while in the first of Chronicles (xxi. 11–12) we read, 'Thus saith the Lord, Choose thee either *three* years of famine.' To keep to the same event—in the second of Samuel (xxiv. 24) David, we are told, paid for the threshing floor over which the plague stopped 'fifty shekels of silver.' In the first of Chronicles (xxi. 25) the price paid is said to have been '*six hundred* shekels of *gold*.'

That some of these apparent contradictions may be explained by the mistakes of transcribers as to letters used to express numeral powers, or by the accidental addition or omission of a cipher, is probable enough; but let that be as it may, it is as certain that they exist, as it is that they relate only to matters of detail, and have no bearing whatever on moral or religious truth. To deny these discrepancies, or to explain them away in an unsatisfactory manner, is only to confirm unbelievers in their incredulity. To shut one's eyes to them is mere stupidity. It is to say in effect that if we refuse to see a fact we shall not come into collision with it, which is simply as untrue as it is absurd. As the Bishop of London has well remarked: 'When laborious ingenuity has exerted itself to collect a whole store of such difficulties, supposing them to be real, what on earth does it signify? They may quietly float away without our being able to solve them, if we bear in mind the acknowledged fact that there is a human element in the Bible.'

They are, however, certainly fatal to those who assert that 'not only is the Word of God in the Bible, but the Bible is itself, in the strictest and fullest sense, in every particular of its contents, and in every expression which it uses, the infallible word of the one living and true God.' Just as, in like manner, the voice of the rocks must eventually cover with confusion all who are unwise enough to say that 'the Bible could not reveal spiritual truth infallibly, unless it were infallible also in all that it says about physical truth; in other words, that all its references to physical truths must be true, God being, if without offence it may be thus spoken, responsible for them.' This ground is taken by Mr. Burgon, Dr. Candlish, and others.

But the fact is, Scripture nowhere puts forward any such claim. If it did it would be a thing of 'the letter' rather than of 'the spirit,' and the least flaw in expression would be fatal to its pretensions. Again, if inspiration were in the letter, it is not easy to see how the book could be translated without being destroyed: whereas, as a fact, it passes into every tongue, and is, when faithfully rendered, quite as much the Word of God in one language as in another. Further, the apostles not unfrequently quote *the sense* of a passage rather than its exact words; in this, as in other ways, *leaving the impression* that the infallible Word of God is to be found only in that body of doctrine, whether prophetic or preceptive, which they had received from above; *connected, indeed*, but not to be confounded, with the history of their nation, the character of their literature, or the experience of their lives.

On the other hand, to concede the fact that the sacred writers were only inspired to teach *Divine truth*, and that in other matters they are left to their natural faculties as honest witnesses, far from weakening the cause of Scripture, goes directly to deprive the objector of his most dangerous weapon. 'The spiritual element in Scripture—that is, everything in it which concerns our relation to God and to eternity—though combined with other elements, *is plainly distinguishable from them*, and wholly independent of them; and since the evidence of Christianity attaches infallibility only to the spiritual element, the discovery of errors in the Bible does not touch Christianity at all.'[1]

That the *structure* of the Bible, the marvellous unity which subsists between all its parts—the reverberation, so to speak, of one great truth through all its pages, from Genesis to the Apocalypse—affords strong ground for believing that its production, *as a whole*, is, in a certain sense, the work of the Divine mind, providentially guiding each writer, compiler, or editor, to one great end, we are far from disputing; but this fact, while it most clearly and distinctly separates the Book from all mere human compositions, and while it should guard us against the folly implied in asserting that this or that is superfluous, by no means proves that everything it contains is divinely inspired, and therefore infallibly true, or that *in all its parts* it is 'profitable for doctrine, for reproof, for correction, or for instruction in righteousness.' The treasure is in earthen vessels in more senses than one, and this simply because it is on the whole *best* that it should be so.

Yet it should not be forgotten that while, as a rule, truth revealed by God to man is to be found in the spirit rather than in the letter, for Divine thoughts are always 'Spirit and Life,' the literal cannot always be dispensed with. The prophecies which declare at once the greatness and the lowliness of Messiah were evidently intended to be understood literally, so many of them having been *literally* fulfilled. A prophecy, indeed, can scarcely be said to be fulfilled at all which is not, to some extent at least, fulfilled to the letter. If God did not literally 'bring a flood of waters upon the earth to

[1] Byrne's Donnellan Lectures before the University of Dublin.

destroy all flesh wherein is the breath of life from under heaven,' the announcement that He would do so is untrustworthy. But if He did, it is comparatively of little consequence *how* the event was brought about, or whether the waters did or did not cover the whole earth.

Why, then, should we be so anxious regarding the literal accuracy, for instance, of everything in the Pentateuch? Why should we be troubled if we find it impossible to reconcile the two accounts of the creation given in the first and second chapters of Genesis, and therefore come to the conclusion that it is needless to enquire whether they record the same event, or whether, as some suppose, the former relates to a race that passed away long before Adam was born? Why should we be at all careful to decide whether the 'six days' spoken of mean six of our days, or whether they represent periods of long or short duration? whether the narrative of the Fall is to be understood literally, or whether it in any degree involves allegory or other figure of speech? Why should we be concerned to know whether by the term 'Sons of God' in the sixth chapter, the pious descendants of Seth are meant, or whether, as the late Dr. Maitland has maintained in his 'Eruvin,' other intelligences, with whom we have now no possibility of contact, are intended? Why should we even stop to enquire within what limits the entrance of animals into the Ark is to be confined, or yet whether the Flood itself overflowed the whole globe, or only those portions of it which were then inhabited?

These questions are not unimportant. They all have their place in Biblical criticism, and they have all been treated, if not invariably with wisdom, certainly with abundant learning. But, settle them as we may, the value of the document out of which they spring is undiminished. So far as any man's trust in the Bible is concerned, it matters very little whether this or that portion of the narrative is to be understood literally or figuratively. The one sole question in which he is interested is this, Can the record be depended upon? is it *essentially* truthful?

Literality is certainly not in itself essential to truthfulness. The parables of the Lord are quite as true as any other parts of His teaching; and figures of speech may sometimes express truth in all its fulness and completeness, better than any simple and literal statements could do. The book of Genesis was not written for Englishmen only, nor yet for the men of the nineteenth century alone. It has no exclusive message to the practical, the scientific, the learned. It is addressed to men of all ages, of all temperaments, in all the various stages of civilization and of culture, and the problem to be solved in producing a written account of the origin of the world was this: How can the information be best communicated so as to be equally adapted to the condition and necessities of each and all? It may be that this could be effected only by divergence from the literal, by the occasional use of a form of speech more likely to convey a *true impression* than any plain, prosaic, matter of fact statement could possibly do. Be this, however, as it may, the value of the Bible is by no means dependent on these things; and one scarcely knows which most to wonder at—the malice which rejoices to declare that the authority of Scripture is overthrown if a discrepancy can be discovered, or the folly of those Christians who seem to stake Divine revelation itself on the verbal accuracy of either text or translation.

We ask not, then, whether the 'bow' in heaven first became visible after the Flood, or whether, as previously existing, it was only appropriated as the token of the covenant made with the earth; whether literally men thought to build a tower that should reach unto heaven, or whether the 'city and tower' spoken of ought not to be regarded as a symbolic expression of the fact that a great ungodly centralisation was now attempted; whether the confusion of tongues, although in the first instance judicial and special, was, as to its perpetuation, anything more or different from that tendency—perpetually manifested where no common centre exists, and where communication is infrequent—to vary and corrupt a language until it becomes absolutely unintelligible to those who once in common terms expressed their wants and wishes.

None of these questions need we care to have answered, simply because, as we have before said, the truthfulness of the narrative does not depend on its literality. Expound these matters as we may, the record still stands, the only record that can be regarded as furnishing even a plausible account of the world's history prior to the calling of Abram. And this is equally true in relation to the entire Pentateuch. What does it matter whether Moses was directly inspired to write all that is found therein, or whether he was divinely commissioned to condense and to correct fragments of earlier documents, and to give shape to the memory of traditions otherwise sure to pass away? What does it matter whether these writings were or were not at a later period re-edited with additions? Of one thing we may be quite sure, viz. that Moses did not write the account of his own death.

What if many of the numbers given in Exodus should, as Bishop Colenso asserts, be inaccurate? What is to be gained by assertions or denials relative to matters which have for ever passed out of the reach of our verification? What if, here and there, a law should seem to us strange and unaccountable; an event difficult to comprehend; a statement to involve an apparent contradiction? What has all this to do with the essential value of the Book? Absolutely nothing; unless thereby its truthfulness can be set aside.

If, indeed, Moses never existed, being only a myth; if no deluge ever took place; if the children of Israel were not led out of Egypt by the special interference of God; if the supernatural element can be altogether discharged, either as fraudulent imposture or mere delusion: why then certainly the sooner this strange book is buried the better. 'If,' as has been observed by an able writer in Fraser's Magazine, 'the rules of criticism require us to set aside, as fabulous or legendary, the miraculous events related in the Bible, then the only witnesses from whom we learn anything regarding God as revealed to man are so entirely discredited that we cannot trust anything they say. The Apostles' Creed ought in this case to be reduced to the words, "I believe that Jesus Christ was crucified under Pontius Pilate." The rest of the history would become the domain of the historical imagination.'

We now proceed to enquire whether any principle

can be found by the application of which the inspired in Scripture can be separated from the uninspired; and further, whether intelligent and ordinarily educated Christians do or do not possess any faculty by the use of which they can exercise the discrimination needed.

CHAPTER III.

THE VERIFYING FACULTY.

We now approach that portion of our task which demands of us *a principle*, by the help of which we may, without weakening faith in Scripture as a whole, separate its parts, and distinguish between that which is Divine and that which is human.

Such a principle will assuredly not be sought for in vain, if it is recollected that *all inspired Scripture is congruous*; not only in the sense of being in itself suitable and pertinent to the purpose for which it was given, but also as being in harmony with all that is revealed of the character of God. Further—and for this statement we have inspired authority—that the congruity thus existing *is capable of being discerned* by every spiritual man who is faithful to the light bestowed upon him.

If this be granted—and it is difficult to see how the admission can be refused—we have at once *a test* by which everything assumed to be inspired of God may be tried without presumption, and with little probability of mistake.

Before attempting to apply any such test, however, it may be necessary to show that God *intended* that His children should thus discriminate; that He has given them all that is needful for the accomplishment of the work; and, further, that with regard to Scripture, He has made the fulfilment of this duty no unimportant part of their moral probation.

If, therefore, it be said, as it probably will, that any attempt to draw a distinction between different parts of the Bible—to separate the inspired from the uninspired, the Divine from the human—renders the Book as a whole useless to simple Christians, inasmuch as they can perceive no such differences, it is enough to reply that *this is not the fact*, since that which was true of the *oral*, is equally true of the *written* revelation.

The exhortation of the Apostle John to his converts, 'Beloved, believe not every spirit, but try the spirits whether they be of God,' supposes an ability in every spiritually enlightened man, whether hearer or reader, to discern between that which is of God and that which is not. 'Ye have an unction from the Holy One,' says the aged saint, and in the power of this unction, 'ye (the poorest of the flock) know all things.' I myself, he says—and if he, other inspired men also—'have not written unto you because ye know not the truth, but because ye know it. The anointing which ye have received of Him abideth in you, and ye need not that any man teach you' (1 John ii. 20 and 27).

We call this 'the verifying faculty,' and regard it as being neither more nor less than *reason enlightened and sanctified by the Holy Spirit.* To vilify reason, as so many good but ill-instructed Christians do, is a folly which would be unpardonable, if it did not commonly arise from sheer ignorance or weakness of mind. As Butler truly says, 'Reason is the only faculty we have wherewith to judge concerning anything, even revelation itself.' Its duty in relation to Scripture is to judge, 'not whether it contains things *different from what we should have expected* from a wise, just, and good Being, but whether it contains things plainly contradictory to wisdom, justice, or goodness'—in other words, to what elsewhere God teaches us of Himself.

Of course all this goes on the assumption that Divine teaching is addressed to men who have at least some moral sympathy with its utterances; that the words of God are spiritual words; that the sheep *know the voice* of the Good Shepherd. In a limited sense, much of this is true of every book the tendency of which is elevating. All moral teaching worthy of the name addresses itself to the *consciousness* of those to whom it speaks. Only as it comes in contact with a prepared mind; only as it proves an interpreter of floating and half-formed thought, or is the expression of feelings before but partially recognised or understood, does any book of this kind produce permanent impressions, or prove of much real value.

But this is true of the Bible in an altogether preeminent degree; for this book, whether it reveals new truth, or whether it explains a man to himself, is, like the sun in heaven, seen in its own light. Not that all truth is in this way made plain to all persons; but that everything essential to the growth in goodness of the man who reads, is, by a mysterious affinity, recognised and laid hold of for the soul's salvation from evil. The softened heart responds to words which awake no echo in other breasts. It is always so. The words of Him who spake 'as never man spake,' only elicited scorn from the great mass of those who heard them uttered.

The seed and the soil must be adapted to each other, or there can be no living product. The spiritual faculty may be dormant, the 'God-consciousness' all but dead, being completely overridden by 'self-consciousness,' yet the possession of it is always recognised.

It is, indeed, not a little singular that the very Book 'that has had greater influence upon the world than all others,' differs from all others in affirming the darkness of the natural man—that man is spiritually dead, and in making that statement *the basis* of all that it contains respecting the past and present and future of mankind. Still more singular is it, that almost all men feel the truth of the statement, and bow before its declaration that this is not their true life. There is a sense, therefore, in which almost all thoughtful men feel the worth of the Bible; *some of those not least who have most felt themselves compelled to oppose it.* For what book has sounded so the depths of experience, or scaled like it the highest pinnacles of thought? What man has not learnt through it better to know himself?'[1]

The Old Testament is professedly the history of 'a peculiar people.' Its prophecies and its revelations were all but confined to them. The discourses of Jesus, without any exclusion of the many, were, for the most part, addressed to the few. The Epistles were all written to persons acknowledging the Divine authority of the writers. Why, then, should it be thought strange to hold that the same utterances, which were originally addressed only to those who were more or less capable of estimating their value, should still be in harmony with the spiritual intuitions *of those only*

[1] Man and his Dwelling-place: an Essay.

who are prepared to receive them with docility? 'Unto him *that hath* shall be given.' The knowledge of God is not imparted to men as if it were evidence addressed to the senses, nor can it be conveyed by any merely logical process similar to the demonstrations of science. No *moral* truth can be understood until it is appreciated, and to be appreciated *it must be practised.*

That there is a Divine teacher of man's spirit, and that it is possible for a man's spirit to have converse with that teacher, is a truth which would remain true if the Bible and all its revelations were to be annihilated; but the recognition of this truth would still be of no practical use to any man who was unwilling to listen and obey. It matters not whether we call the special faculty by which man attains to a knowledge of the Divine, a spiritual gift or a verifying power; the fact is the same; without it all is dark alike in the Bible and in the highest intuitions of the soul. Tenets may be drawn from Scripture by any man, but living truths only by prepared hearts. It is the forgetfulness or the denial of this fact which renders so much that has been written on 'the verifying faculty' in man unsatisfactory; since, according to the moral state of each individual, does the application of the phrase in question embody a great truth, or involve a pernicious error.

'The conditions which are required for arriving at the knowledge of Divine truth are surely stern conditions! It is a straight and narrow way which leadeth to life! There must be a continual waiting for light; a distrust of our own assumptions; a readiness to be detected in error, certain that God's meaning is infinitely larger than ours, and that other men may perceive an aspect of it which we do not perceive; a belief that He is fulfilling His promise that all shall be taught of Him in ways which we cannot imagine; a dread of shutting out any truth by our impatient notion that it must contradict some other; a determination to maintain what little has been given us in the hope of its expansion, and never to contradict, if we understand ever so little, what may have been given to another; a resolution to hold the ground on which we stand, without judging him if he cannot yet see what this ground is. Hard is it to form these habits of mind. . . I cannot help perceiving that this mind, the mind of the little child, the mind which our Lord demands of us, has been exhibited by many scientific men who have been censured and scorned by the religious world of their day, and has been sadly deficient in their accusers."[1]

Without *spiritual insight*, nothing is discerned which takes hold of the spirit or influences the character. Until this is received, truth itself is but *an opinion* to the man who comes in contact with it. It does not vitalise because it is not itself vital. It is only a human judgment, and, whether true or false, has little if any moral power in it. It is dead, being alone. Not until opinion is transfigured—not until it quickens into life—does it become a truth, and grow, and bring forth fruit.

But another consequence follows. Looked at in this way it is of no moment that either the uninstructed or the instructed man should be able to say regarding each separate passage of Scripture, *this* is inspired, *that* is

[1] The Claims of the Bible and of Science. By the Rev. F. D. Maurice.

not. How can he indeed? The revelation itself is not a thing *apart* from daily life, but *through* its various relations; how, then, *can* any man undertake to separate in each particular the supernatural element from the natural which it irradiates and explains? To regard anything of the kind as necessary either to confidence or to edification is absurd; as absurd, in fact, as it is to maintain that 'we require an exercise of judgment upon the written document before we can allow men to trust in their King and Saviour.' Everyone knows that this is not the fact; that in all time the multitude never have, nor ever can enter upon any such enquiries; that the masses must either believe in Christ directly as an actual person related to them, and recognised by them in their inmost souls, or they will not believe at all. They listen to the announcement that Christ is their Redeemer, and they believe the good news *just in so far as it finds a response in their own spiritual necessities and consciousness.* Into evidence about documents they cannot enter.

And why should they? The analytical chemist, when called upon to do so, separates the constituent parts of the very atmosphere he breathes; but for all the practical purposes of life he well knows that such a process is altogether needless. Forgetful of his science, he rejoices in the free air of heaven just as the peasant does, and thanks God for its vitality. So is it with Scripture. The critic may doubt or may be satisfied as to the precise place which such or such a passage ought or ought not to occupy in relation to other portions of Holy Writ, and there are times and seasons when such considerations are both proper and profitable. But *he* can scarcely be regarded as a wise man who, coming to the Bible for strength or consolation, for instruction in righteousness, or for help in the perfecting of his character, does anything else than open his heart to its divine teachings, and rejoice like a little child in the sunshine it can shed around his path.

If error were in the Bible cunningly interspersed with truth, the case would be different. But it is not so. The Book, as a whole and as it stands, is wholesome and useful; each portion of it has its proper place, and is adequate to fulfil its appointed end. Everything has its purpose to fulfil and its object to accomplish, whether, properly speaking, inspired or not. Nothing may be despised, nothing pronounced superfluous. But everything in the Book does not take hold alike on the heart and conscience. It may be very interesting, as indeed it is, to trace on the map the various journeyings of St. Paul, or the wanderings of the Children of Israel in the wilderness; to note a hundred undesigned coincidences; to study, and try to reconcile two apparently conflicting genealogies; to examine into and to discuss the chronology, the geography, or the natural history of Palestine; all this and much more may be done—and it is fitting that in its time and place it should be done—yet it may be accomplished without the slightest moral or spiritual benefit arising to the man who is thus occupied.

Real benefit can, in such cases, only be derived from connecting the information thus acquired with living truth found elsewhere; by gathering from such research indirect evidence in favor of the Book itself, or pleasing illustrations to be used in its exposition. But this is a very different state of mind from that which is produced by a devout study of Moses and the prophets; of the Psalms; of Isaiah; of the Sermon on the Mount; of the discourses and prayers of our Lord with His apostles; of the scenes of the Crucifixion; of the early history of the Church as given in the Acts or in the Epistles; or of the wondrous visions of the Apocalypse. Criticism, to the uncritical mind, seems in such cases to be an impertinence. The heart opens to the impression such passages produce, as the flower opens to the sun or the earth drinks in the rain of heaven.

Facts, whether past or present, correspond to this view of things.

We have already seen that the first Christians were under the very same obligation to distinguish the voice of God from the voice of man that we are; and since they were enabled to do so only by an endowment common to Christians of all time, and known as 'the witness of the spirit,' they were practically in the same position as ourselves. Even the most orthodox divines are constrained to admit that the Scriptures can only be received on certain conditions, viz., that we are 'satisfied that the books themselves contain nothing obviously *incompatible* with the ascription to their authors of the Divine assistance, but on the contrary are in all respects favourable to the supposition. We want to see,' says Dr. Alexander, 'that they are in harmony with each other; that the statements they contain are credible; that the doctrines they teach are not foolish, immoral, or self-contradictory; that their authors really assumed to be under the Divine direction in what they wrote, and afforded competent proofs of this to those around them.'[1]

[1] Kitto's Bib. Cycl., art. 'Canon.'

But all this clearly supposes the exercise of a verifying faculty.

The facts of the present day, as they come under our own observation, are all confirmatory. It is 'the wise' only who 'understand.' The peasant is, in this respect, often far before the philosopher. Everything depends on the moral condition of the recipient. Who ever knew a man under the dominant influence of pride able either to comprehend or to estimate the moral dignity of humility? When was a supremely selfish man alive to the duty of self-sacrifice? Where do we find men full of ignorance and conceit—to say nothing of spiritual things—able to judge the value of a great work of art, or to pronounce on the merits of some marvellous production of science or of statesmanship?

But here a paradox appears. It is this. The light of which we speak—the quickening and elevating power in the strength of which we are to recognize the Divine—is never attained except by spiritual culture effected through the instrumentality of the revelation itself. The Book to be recognized and obeyed must itself have more or less educated the consciousness which is to accept it. The word is 'the sword of the Spirit,' and the same Lord who says, 'He that is of the truth heareth My voice,' says also, 'I am the Truth.' It follows, therefore, that before any man can judge of truth, he must receive 'the truth,' believe in it, and be, more or less, educated by it.

Yet, after all, this is not more paradoxical than the kindred fact that before a man can judge as to the merits of a great artist, he must, to some extent, be educated by the artist; or, to take a wider illustration, that a man must himself become civilised before he can perceive how great a blessing civilisation is.

That this way of looking at the matter makes the evidence for the truth of the Bible mainly subjective cannot be disputed; but nothing else in the present day appears to have much hold on men. It may indeed seriously be doubted whether it is now possible to bring forward any evidence, in favour of miracles for instance, which could reasonably be expected to satisfy an unconcerned spectator, and still less an opponent.

In the days of our Lord and His apostles, the miracle was evidence that the teacher was from God. Now, the doctrine must give probability to the miracle. The mere fact that 'wonders were wrought' by the apostles, could this be demonstrated, would of itself avail little to convince any man of the truth of what they taught. Nor perhaps *ought* it to be otherwise. It is only when coupled with other considerations, such as the character of the Christian miracles, their simplicity, benevolence, and unselfish ends, that the force of the argument founded on them comes to be felt. Well and wisely has it been remarked that 'the entire series of miracles recorded by the Evangelists, consummated as they were by the miracle of Christ's resurrection, occupy a place of perpetual efficacy in relation separately to each of the great purposes for which the Lord of Life came amongst us, viz. as Saviour of the world, as Redeemer of His people, and as Conqueror in the world of spirits.'[1] In each of these particulars the miracles attest His mission, and are in all respects congruous with His teaching. The *observation* of these characteristics is the result of

[1] Restoration of Belief, p. 265.

the application of 'the verifying faculty' to the miracles of the New Testament generally.

Of all the miracles, however, the resurrection of Christ, involving as it does our own rising again, is *the one* on the fact of which most turns; for resurrection does not signify *existence elsewhere* under different conditions—it is the renewal of the old. It is the reconstitution of humanity, accompanied in each individual by a sense of identity: with the remembrance of a past, as well as the consciousness of a future. Everything in Christianity hangs on the resurrection of Christ. 'It knows Christ only as risen: the only reason of its own existence that it recognises is the resurrection. The only claim the apostles set forth for preaching it is, that their Master who was crucified was alive once more.' No supposed delusion can account for this belief that Christ rose from the dead. If that which is asserted in Scripture regarding it be not true, the whole is a rank imposture. Either there was a crucified and risen Christ *long before* any part of the New Testament was written, or the book that asserts this to have been the case is a fraud. The New Testament emphatically is based on Christ, not Christ on it.

It may indeed be said that, in relation to miracle, there is no room for the exercise of a verifying faculty, since miracles are simply *impossible*, the laws of nature being incapable of violation. If it be so, the laws of nature are more powerful than their Creator, which is simply absurd.

One thing, however, is quite certain—the admission of the supernatural is essential to the acceptance of any Divine revelation whatever; for revelation, if anything at all, is itself a miracle. Christianity being what it is, and its announcements what they profess to be, 'miracles are necessary to the justification of such announcements, which indeed, unless they are supernatural truths, are the wildest delusions.' A man's faith in the Bible may not indeed *consciously* rest on miracles, but it cannot be a genuine faith unless he admits their reality, since, if not true, the assertion of them discredits everything else that the book contains.

Yet why should so much be said about miracles being violations of law? It is by no means so clear that a miracle *is* a violation of law. 'We ourselves,' says a recent writer, 'formerly had no belief in miracles, because we saw no evidence of supernatural powers working in the natural world; but when asked if we had ever seriously looked for any evidence of this kind, we were obliged to confess we had not; and were astonished to find that, *on seeking with a will*, there was abundant evidence in the history of humanity. . . . The action of supernatural forces upon mind and matter is necessarily as simple and as much in harmony with general laws as the action of natural forces upon mind and matter; the only difference being that the actors in one case are inhabitants of this natural world, while, in other cases, they are inhabitants of the supernatural world.

'Those who refuse to look for evidence of supernatural forces and phenomena, delude themselves and their followers by a false play of words. They very properly refuse to credit stories about "arbitrary interferences with eternal laws of nature;" and then most improperly presume not only to know which are and which are not eternal laws of nature, but also to affirm that all miraculous and supernatural phenomena must necessarily be "arbitrary interferences with eternal laws."

'If a man kills a bird, or causes a tree to wither and die by the aid of natural forces, it is *not* deemed an arbitrary interference; but if Christ causes a barren fig tree to wither and die by the aid of supernatural forces, *it is* an arbitrary interference with eternal laws. If a man is struck dead by lightning it is not an arbitrary interference; but if Ananias fall dead at the feet of the Apostle Peter it is an arbitrary interference and therefore incredible. Such modes of reasoning engender pestilent fallacies. It is well known that superior forces can displace inferior forces without any arbitrary interference with immutable laws; and therefore the real question to be examined is, *the existence of supernatural forces and phenomena*, whether in accordance with known or unknown laws."[1]

Yet even here discrimination is needed. If the tendency of some minds is to universal scepticism in relation to the supernatural, that of others is to the credulous acceptance of almost everything professing to be of this character. Hence the necessity for a verifying faculty in man, which, apart altogether from ordinary investigation, should judge that which professes to be spiritual by a spiritual standard. 'False prophets,' says our Lord to His disciples 'shall arise, *and shall show great signs and wonders*; insomuch that, if it were possible, they shall deceive the very elect' (Matt. xxiv. 24). St. John in the Apocalypse, too,

[1] Philosophy of Religion. By Hugh Doherty, M. D.

however obscurely, speaks of a time when 'spirits of devils' (demons) will go forth 'working miracles' (Rev. xvi. 14). Again, he describes an apostate who should 'deceive them that dwell on the earth by the means of those *miracles which he had power to do'* (Rev. xiii. 14). The security against such deceivers is not to be found in scepticism—for sceptics are often singularly credulous, and commonly more or less superstitious—but in that verifying faculty which is by John identified with the 'anointing' Christians receive from Him who abideth in them.

That, as a rule, mankind should be only too ready to believe in the supernatural is not surprising. *The great silence of God* when oppression and wrong are rampant in the earth, is often a severe trial to the faith even of the best. Hence the singular proneness of most persons to judge hastily, and to interpret rashly both providences and predictions. The human mind cannot be bounded by time; it ever longs to pierce the invisible. Here, too, therefore, is to be found abundant scope for the exercise of that spiritual insight which is the true verifying faculty, as much when it restrains as when it enlightens.

CHAPTER IV.

MANY AUTHORS, BUT ONE BOOK.

We propose now to revert to a peculiarity of the Bible which was incidentally referred to in a preceding chapter, but not dwelt upon as it deserves to be, viz., the *marvellous unity* which subsists between its different parts.

Scripture, as we all know, is a collection of tracts, the work of above thirty authors, who utter what they have to say, not contemporaneously, but in succession, and along a vast line of time, say 1,600 years. Yet, in spite of this, we all feel it to be ONE BOOK. We do so because, explain it as we may, we see, as Mr. De Quincy says, that 'all the writers combine to one end, and lock, like parts of a great machine, into one system.' On this peculiarity the argument has been founded—and it is a weighty one—that inasmuch as concert in the writers was impossible, the unity in question places the Bible in a position altogether distinct from that of any other book; and seems at least to justify the assumption that its preparation under Divine direction is, in some sense or other, and in a very high sense too, a great fact.

We turn to the Book, then, in order to discover whether that which has been asserted regarding its unity amid diversity is true, or only a fancy.

The first sentence that meets the eye consists of ten pregnant words: 'In the beginning God created the heavens and the earth;' words that involve an utter denial of the Pagan doctrine of the eternity of matter, and an equally positive denial of the Pantheistic theory that God is but the soul of the universe. For they affirm most positively: first, that in some far distant period—how distant we know not—the world in which we live had a beginning; and next, that He who created it is altogether distinct from it, a personal God, endowed with Almighty power and infinite wisdom. On this assertion all subsequent revelation clearly proceeds.

The successive stages of that wondrous process, by which order sprang out of chaos, light out of darkness, and sea and land, sun and moon, grass and herb, beast and fowl, and finally man and woman, came into existence, is next brought under notice. Then follows the story of the Garden and the Fall; the expulsion from Eden; the birth of Cain; the murder of Abel; the longevity and rapid increase of mankind; the equally rapid growth of wickedness; and, after abundant warning, the final destruction of a sinful race in waters from which Noah and his family are alone preserved.

Other records of the world's earliest history have we none. The question is therefore an important one, Can this be depended upon? The momentous point is, *not* whether everything recorded is to be taken in its most literal acceptation, for this, we have already seen, is not essential to trustworthiness; but whether the narrative can be depended upon *in that higher sense* which implies *the truest impression* that, under the circumstances, could be produced on mankind as a whole. This is essential. If a writer intentionally leaves a false impression, his work is fraudulent and worthless. Further, if a narrative be in spirit untrue, nothing stable can be built upon it; for what is any erection worth that rests only on a quicksand? But—and to this attention should be specially directed—the narrative before us is either *a foundation* or it is nothing. All that follows evidently rests upon it. Its essential accuracy is taken for granted by every subsequent writer, and if the truthfulness of it be even doubtful, the entire volume of revelation is doubtful too.

Let us take, then, first, the seven brief chapters of whose contents we have been speaking, and examine them narrowly. In doing this it is scarcely possible to fail in perceiving two leading elements: an *historic* element mingling with a didactic one; and a *supernatural* element involving both miraculous occurrences and predictions relating to the future.

The *first element* (the historic) embraces the actual narrative regarded as true, and *equally true*, whether any portion of it be veiled in allegory or not, whether it be a literal narrative, or only 'an inspired psalm of creation.' The didactic associated with it, is involved in passages such as those which deny the eternity of matter; affirm the personality of the Creator; imply a day of rest; or exhibit the probationary character of human existence, as it appears in *the test* to which our first parents were subjected, and in the *great lesson* involved therein, that he who had just been created in the image of God, and invested with power over every living thing, must, before he could govern well, learn implicitly to obey; in *the relation* established between man and woman; in *the representation* given us of the tempter, viz., as an animal only, endowed indeed with high intellect, but without a ruling conscience, without any sense of duty, or anything corresponding to unselfish affection; in *the trial* of obedience being found, not in one great act of self-sacrifice, but in daily and hourly resistance to temptation regarding an apparent trifle, and this *without being able to perceive* the reason or the usefulness of the self-denial demanded; in *the retribution* which follows sin; in the *communication of an evil nature* to descendants; in the institution of sacrifices, bloody or unbloody; and in the final sweeping away of the wicked from the earth they had filled with violence. These are the great lessons which, embodied in the history, form what may be called the didactic element.

The *second* (the supernatural) is seen in the original act of creation, in the temptation by a speaking serpent, and in the desolations of the flood.

Now, as we advance, we shall have to notice how these combined elements go to make up all that we regard as sacred writings, whether directly inspired or only providentially preserved; how they run through each separate portion of the books, and how each of these elements in particular connects itself with that which has gone before. It will soon be obvious that the value or worthlessness of all that is uttered depends entirely on the truthfulness, or otherwise, of the basis on which it rests.

We pass on, therefore, to the consideration of the new world as it emerges from the waters. God remembers Noah; the windows of heaven are closed; the waters subside; the Ark rests on Ararat, and its inmates come forth. In process of time Ham is cursed and Shem and Japheth blessed. Again mankind multiply; a great empire springs into existence; language is confounded, and nations, differing in speech, plant themselves in all parts of the earth.

The elements already noticed reappear. The *historic* runs through the whole, whether certain portions be regarded as literal or figurative. The didactic mingling therewith appears in the recognition of seven days as a division of time; in the renewal of sacrifice; in the forbidding to eat anything while living; in the declaration that whoso sheddeth man's blood, by man shall his blood be shed; in the command to be fruitful and multiply, sanctifying marriage; and in the drunkenness of Noah, inculcating moderation and circumspection in the use even of Divine gifts. The *supernatural* is seen in the safety of the Ark and its inhabitants, and in the preservation and distribution of the animals. The predictive, as a branch of the supernatural, appears in the curse on Canaan, and in the blessing on his brethren.

Here, then, we have *the second course of stones*, so to speak, needful to the formation of that great mystical temple of truth, which is now rising from the ground; and nothing can be more obvious than that this second course rests upon, and dovetails into, the first.

The calling of Abram, that of him might be made a great nation; the story of his wanderings; the history of Isaac and Jacob; and the settlement in Egypt, bring us to the close of the book of Genesis. Need it be said that this gives us, in the form of history, the only account of patriarchal times that the world possesses? And how wonderfully vivid and natural it is! What light it throws on the early movements of mankind; upon the birth of empires; upon the moral state of a race living chiefly on traditions! What pictures of a nomadic life, not so very different from that of the modern Arab of the desert! What an insight into the Egypt of antiquity! What a photograph of the world as it was four thousand years ago!

In the didactic portion let us observe the character and elevation of the teaching. First, the danger as well as sin of deceit and falsehood is exemplified in Abram's duplicity both towards Pharaoh and the king of Gerar; in Isaac's conduct under similar circumstances; in Jacob's dealings with Esau; and in Rebekah's treachery towards her husband. Let us observe, too, how the sin in each case involves a cowardly distrust of God, and an attempt to justify the evil on the ground that good would come of it, as if the Divine purposes could either be forwarded or thwarted by human fraud and deceit.

Next we may observe how the duty of unselfishness, of *yielding* rather than striving even for a right, is exemplified by Abraham in his dealings with Lot, and by Isaac with the herdmen of Gerar. Then we have the folly of worldliness exhibited in Lot's selection of a dwelling-place, without regard to its moral atmosphere, while the power of faith and the beauty of self-sacrifice is seen in the offering of Isaac.[1] The spirit of a dignified

[1] '*The offering*'—i. e. the giving him up cheerfully to God either for life or death. The word 'offering' (*olah*), it has been suggested, does not necessarily imply a 'burnt offering,' as our translators have it. And it is certainly worth notice that no command is given to Abraham to slay his son, or to take with him wood, or fire, or

liberality is manifested by Abraham in the purchase of the field of Ephron the Hittite; his disinterestedness in his conduct after the victory over the kings; and his prudent forethought in the marriage of Isaac. The odiousness of oppression comes out in the history of Laban's transactions with Jacob; of cruelty in the con-

knife. Abraham, doubtless, *inferred* that God intended him to kill his child, and he was ready for the sacrifice, 'accounting that God was able to raise him up even from the dead, from whence also he received him in a figure.' But this does not prove that the inference was a right one. It certainly seems incredible that God should, under any circumstances, or for any purpose, command Abraham to imitate the heathen, and bid him do an act which He Himself subsequently pronounced an abomination (Deut. xii. 31). That the patriarch was not permitted to carry out his intentions is only what might have been expected; while the spirit of faith, obedience, and self-sacrifice, which was involved in his *willingness* to resign Isaac, was not the less approved and rewarded.

Another suggestion has been thrown out by Dean Stanley, viz., the possibility that the impression Abraham received that God wished him to slay his son, although permitted and overruled, came from Satan rather than from the Lord; that Satan's design was to show, as in the case of Job, that there was a limit beyond which Abraham's faith and obedience would not go—the result proving the sincerity and the power of the godly man's faith, for the exercise of which he was blessed of God more emphatically than ever. This theory is supposed to find support from the fact that in the second book of Samuel (xxiv. 1) the Lord is said to have moved David to say, 'Go, number Israel and Judah,' while the same act is in the first book of Chronicles (xxi. 1) attributed to Satan: 'And Satan stood up against Israel, and provoked David to number Israel.' It is every way uncandid and unworthy of a Christian man to assume that either of these suppositions has originated in a sinful unwillingness to receive Bible statements as they stand. Rather are they occasioned by a holy fear of attributing to God a command to do anything which He Himself has pronounced evil.

duct of Simeon and Levi toward the Shechemites. The nobility of forgiveness is shown by Esau when he meets his brother; the power of prayer in the intercession of Abram for Sodom, and in the mystic wrestle of Jacob with the angel; and, finally, the retributive justice of God in the sorrows of Jacob, and in the distress of Joseph's brethren when brought before his face in Egypt. To say that this teaching is elevated is to say little. To suppose that it is the work of any fraudulent person, imposing upon the world a pretended revelation, is simply extravagant and absurd.

The predictive element enlarges as we proceed. In the covenant with Abraham; in the promise made to him and to his descendants; in the various renewals of the covenant; in the dying blessings of Isaac and Jacob; in the childish dreams of Joseph about himself and his brethren; and in his later prophecies regarding the butler and the baker, and respecting the seven years' famine, we see the same claim to the power of foreseeing future events put forward, which we observed in the earlier portion. The supernatural, in all its forms, rather increases than diminishes. The plaguing of Pharaoh's house on account of Sarah; the appearance and conversation of the angels at the door of Abram's tent; the destruction of Sodom and Gomorrah; the smoking furnace and the burning lamp; the birth of Isaac; the vision of Abimelech; the voice to Hagar; Jacob's dream at Haran; his vision of God's host; and, above all, the marvellous separation of this one family from all other peoples, are events which, if in any sense true, are certainly supernatural.

Observe, too, how all these events grow naturally out

of those that had preceded them. The tendency to corruption after the deluge had been shown at Babel; it had, as the nations multiplied, spread far and wide; it was needful that this tendency should be corrected, for there was a modified idolatry even in a family like Laban's, and atrocious wickedness had been manifested in Sodom and Gomorrah. The world was morally sinking, yet it had not altogether sunk, for both Pharaoh and Abimelech fear God; Melchisedek is a patriarchal priest, before whom Abraham bows; and Joseph though a prince of Egypt, recognises and serves the God of his fathers. The very wickedness that is committed by the various members or connections of the chosen family: the incest of Lot; the treacherous murder of the Shechemites in revenge for the violence of the son of Hamor; the sin of Reuben; the selling of Joseph by his brethren; their falsehood to their father; the disobedience of Er and Onan; the wickedness of Judah, and the folly of Tamar, all testify to a state of society precisely such as might be anticipated on the supposition that the world was exactly what it is stated to be. As Cain and Abel were but types of classes of their descendants, so Shem and Ham continually repeat themselves in the best and in the worst of their race. *The third course of stones*, then, fits exactly to the second, and must stand or fall with its predecessors.

We hasten on to the exodus of the chosen people; to their wanderings through the desert; to the establishment of the ceremonial law; and to their settlement in Canaan under the leadership of Joshua. This brings us to the end of the Pentateuch. Is this also, we ask, dependent upon the preceding? Assuredly it is. All the events narrated spring out of that which has gone before, and cannot by any stretch of ingenuity be explained without it.

The same elements again appear. The historic, whether the narrative in all its details is always accurate or not. The didactic, in the addition to the great moral principles laid down in former portions, of a code of laws adapted to the particular necessities of a peculiar people. The predictive, in the song of blessing by Moses, and in the utterances of Balaam. In a certain sense, indeed, the entire ceremonial law, its sacrifices, its washings, its symbolic worship, all involve a predictive element; for they all seem to point to something better than themselves, which in due time should be manifested on the earth. The *supernatural* is indeed everywhere. The plagues of Egypt; the passage of the Red Sea; the fall of the manna; the flight of quails; the water gushing from the rock; the giving of the law at Mount Sinai; the deaths of Dathan and Abiram, and of Nadab and Abihu; the pillar of cloud by day and of fire by night; the leprosy of Miriam; the fiery serpents; the cure of the people; and the burial of Moses by the Lord Himself: all these things come before us, in a form which obliges us either to regard them as supernatural events, or, for there is no medium, as pure fictions—falsehoods imposed for truth on the credulity of mankind; and if so, they are fatal to the character of the entire book in which they are found.

We have seen, then, that the Pentateuch, however composed, is unquestionably a unity; that whether it is to be invariably regarded as a literal record of events or not, it is essentially historic; that its morality is of the highest; its general truthfulness self-evident; its simplicity and beauty unrivalled; and, further, that it everywhere involves the supernatural. But there is nothing that can make against the supposition that side by side with certain distinct and positive Divine revelations, are found documents providentially selected and edited, but not inspired. The predictive element, if accepted at all, obliges us to admit the supernatural process which we call inspiration, and, in so doing, the supernatural element generally. The narrative, on the other hand, however historically true, need not for many reasons be regarded as in all respects infallible. Jewish history, notwithstanding its being found in the Bible, is but history after all, and must be judged by a very different standard from that which belongs to directly inspired communications. We accept it, rather in consequence of the connection in which it stands, and the general character of the book in which it is embodied, than on account of any direct proof we can by possibility have of its entire accuracy.

But this is of little moment, so long as we feel confident that it is truthful, and can regard it, in that character, as a stable foundation for what follows. Short of an absolute denial of the supernatural in all its forms, which is simply to deny or to limit God, to refuse Him the character of a free agent, and to cut Him off altogether from direct communication with the creatures He has made, it is impossible to find any good or reasonable ground for denying the general credibility of the Pentateuch. But so long as we retain belief in a God at all—that is to say, in a personal God, having a character, and therefore capable of being known and loved—the *possibility* at least of the supernatural must be admitted. On the other hand, 'If Christianity be true historically, its miracles included, and if indeed "Christ rose from the dead according to the Scriptures," then the writings which bring such facts as these to our knowledge will take a place of *authority* in our mind and conscience which, practically, and as to their influence in determining our faith and our conduct, *must be very nearly the same, whatever may be the theory or the opinion we adopt* among the many that have been advanced *concerning inspiration*."[1]

That the later historic portions of the Bible are based upon the Pentateuch, that they presuppose the authority of the books of Moses, will probably not be disputed. Joshua at Shechem recapitulates the leading events therein related as the well-known national history of the people he is addressing. Others in after times take the same course. Not a hint of the possible untrustworthiness of these traditions or documents is to be found anywhere. On the contrary, they are always regarded as sacred, and they are preserved for the most part with a veneration which sometimes degenerates into superstition.

Equally obvious is it that the same characteristics which belong to the earlier documents distinguish those that follow. The message, whatever it may be, is always identical in tone and spirit with that of the five books. The voice of the one is the voice of the other. The historic, the didactic, the predictive and the miraculous all in turn reappear, and as a rule under the same

[1] The Restoration of Belief, p. 238.

conditions. Nothing can be plainer than that, whether true or false, the later documents are but the natural and necessary outgrowth of those which have preceded them.

CHAPTER V.

JEWISH HISTORY AND PROPHECY.

Jewish history, although the history of a peculiarly governed people, and therefore of times in which God *more obviously* interfered with human affairs than He now does, is, as has been already observed, but history after all; and there is not a hint in Scripture which should lead us to imagine that it was composed under any other conditions than those which belong to the historian everywhere, who seeks and finds providential guidance in his work.

We have a right, indeed, to suppose that the men who, under a theocracy,[1] were officially called to write or to edit the transactions of the nation, were truthful men, honourable and honoured by their countrymen, and endowed with high talent if not with special gifts

[1] '*Under a theocracy.*'—This phrase is often supposed to imply more than it really does. The theocratic form of government under which the Jews long lived by no means involved either *a continual miraculous interference* on their behalf, or preservation from any of the errors to which mankind are liable. Rather was it *such a presence among them* as *admitted the possibility*—whenever they were in a right state of mind—of the will of God being ascertained on any given question. When they neglected or ceased to care for Divine direction it was obviously withheld. Scripture affords abundant proof that even before the monarchy the people were often left to their own devices.

from above. We know that some of them were so. Samuel, Nathan, Gad, Isaiah, and Jeremiah, although sometimes historians, were also prophets, men richly endowed with high moral and spiritual qualifications. Of Iddo, Ahijah, and Shemaiah; of the men who wrote, or compiled, or condensed from more extended records, the books of the Kings and Chronicles, we know less. But of this we are assured, that, whether accomplished by Ezra or by any other hand, the grand outline we have of the history of the ancient people is *a compilation* from documents long since lost; drawn up doubtless for religious ends and under the guidance of a wise Providence, but never pretending to the character of a Divine revelation. It is surely but wilfulness or folly to give to these records, invaluable as they are, a character which they themselves do not claim, or to say of them, what has never been said of any other history, that every particular must be infallibly true, or the entire document is false and worthless.

That some of these books *embody* Divine revelations is clear enough, if we accept as truthful the frequently recurring declaration, 'Thus saith the Lord,' or 'The Lord said unto me,' phrases which, when connected with direct communications from above, must certainly be understood to imply that the speaker *claims* Divine authority for what he is saying, and this not the less because similar expressions are at other times not unfrequently used in a lower sense, viz. as indicating that the writer or speaker believes himself to be uttering that which is in accordance with the Divine will. Instances of such use may be found in the address of Joshua (xxiv. 2) where he is plainly recapitulating history, and again in the speech of Jotham (Judg. ix. 6–8). David also in speaking of Shimei exclaims, 'The Lord *hath said* unto him, Curse David' (2 Sam. xvi. 10), evidently meaning the Lord permitted him thus to act. Some of the books, indeed, such as those of Esther and of Ruth, contain nothing which could not have been written without special assistance by any competent person acquainted with the facts; yet these books are *essential* to the completeness of Scripture, and as such are greatly to be prized. To insist that they are inspired adds nothing to their value. It is but to maintain, what every page of Holy Scripture contradicts, that God works miraculously when ordinary agencies are every way adequate to the accomplishment of the end sought.

There is not, within the whole compass of Scripture, a word to show that Jewish history is inspired in the only sense in which that word ought to be used, viz. in the sense of the writers having what they wrote supernaturally revealed to them, and their being, as a consequence, infallible. The marvellous fidelity with which the faults and the crimes of the greatest and best of the kings are recorded, however humbling to the individual whose life is described, or to Israel as a nation, certainly indicates in the writers a subjection to truth and to God perhaps nowhere else to be met with; but this is no evidence of Divine inspiration, inasmuch as that which they were called upon to record was not the result of any special Divine communication, but related to matters within human cognizance, and therefore attainable by care and industry.

We have said that 'Jewish history, notwithstanding its being found in the Bible, is but history after all.'[1]

[1] Chap. iv. p. 101; and also chap. v. p. 104.

and, so far as the facts themselves are concerned, this is true. It must not, however, be forgotten that the annals in question differ from all others in a particular which frequently involves the presence of an inspired element. They not only narrate facts—they *reveal motives* ; they sometimes assert that such or such a transaction took place for reasons which could only be known to the Searcher of Hearts ; they profess at other times to tell us authoritatively *how* such transactions were viewed by God, and what relation they had to the secret history, the sins or the follies of the actors.

In ordinary history these things are concealed. The motives which have led a man to any given course of conduct may, indeed, often be *surmised*, but they cannot be *known*. The light in which a particular action is viewed by the Divine Being may frequently be *inferred* from what we know of His character ; but inasmuch as acquaintance with many circumstances connected with its performance are almost always out of our reach, the inference may be a wrong one. To God alone it belongs to weigh spirits and to discern the thoughts and intents of the heart. With Him, therefore, exclusively rests the ability to form just judgments, or at least to be assured that they are so.

In Jewish history no room is left for doubt of this kind. *There* the most secret thoughts of a man are, not always indeed, but oftentimes, unveiled ; the most plausible pretences are laid bare, and the most positive decisions are given as to the moral quality of the transaction recorded. In such cases we are left in no uncertainty as to the view God takes of an action, or as to the judgment He pronounces upon it.

All this, of course, implies that however human or fallible the narrative itself may be, inspiration is more or less diffused throughout *every part of sacred history which is intended to show forth the living God moving and acting* for definite ends among the children of men.

But this is not all. These annals teach us much that otherwise we could not know. They reveal to us the great truth that not in Judea only, but in all the world, God is ever present; that whether we discern His Hand or not, His power, His wisdom, and His love are perpetually manifested in the lives both of nations and individuals; that a great Divine purpose runs through the ages; that the Controller of all human affairs, however apparently silent, is never absent from the world He has created, never regardless of what is going on upon its surface.

Without this light we should not have been able to discern the Divine working in many cases where it is now quite obvious to us; we should frequently have failed to arrive at either wise or safe conclusions regarding many things that are now made plain; we should perhaps have doubted altogether whether the Lord was indeed ruling among the nations.

It is this *diffused* element in the Bible that gives to the Book the importance it possesses. It is this breathing of the Divine—a peculiarity shared by none other—that justifies the Regal demand it makes on the submission of men to its decisions. Nothing is more certain than that if we study the Old Testament aright we shall find—as Mr. Maurice well says in his dedication to Mr. Erskine of a series of admirable sermons on the Prophets and Kings, which he published about fifteen years ago

—that therein is to be read 'an interpretation of some of the greatest difficulties in history, and in the condition of the world around us.'

We must not omit to observe that there appears throughout the history *a spirit of prophecy which by no means involves Divine inspiration*, and which is quite distinct from that power of predicting future events which belonged to so many of the Hebrew seers. Deborah, Hannah, Saul, nay, whole schools of prophets, from time to time appear upon the scene; some, 'like the wife of Lapidoth, who, in her song over Sisera, strangely intermingling human passion with Divine thanksgiving, expresses the popular feeling without much regard to the propriety or impropriety of the sentiments uttered; some, like the youthful warrior who chants his ode on the dead Saul, apparently blind to the errors of the departed king, and attributes to his hero qualities partaking far more of poetic license than of literal truthfulness;' some, like Hannah, rising out of rejoicings over personal mercies into noble strains wherewith to recount the goodness of Him, 'who keepeth the feet of His saints, breaketh in pieces His adversaries, and exalteth the horn of his anointed;' others, like the crowd who gathered about Ahab at Samaria and bade him go up to Ramoth Gilead, are spoken of as filled with a lying spirit, prophesying for mere gain, 'a crust of bread;' sewing 'pillows under the arm-holes' of the people, and deluding them to their ruin. Here at least any inspiration from above is out of the question.

Not so with other portions. As we advance we come in contact with ruling men who, like Elijah, Elisha, and other less known seers, are obviously the commissioned servants of the Most High, bidden to speak before kings and peoples in words not their own, but God's, and called for the most part to seal their testimony with their blood. By these the faults both of the people and their rulers—their idolatries, their cruelties, their superstitions—are unsparingly exposed, and the calamities that retributively followed their sins are always recognised as Divine judgments, and fulfilments of Mosaic predictions such as those with which the book of Deuteronomy closes.

The constant theme of these men is, 'To what purpose is the multitude of your sacrifices unto me? saith the Lord. Wash you, make you clean; put away the evil of your doings from before Mine eyes; cease to do evil; learn to do well' (Isa. i. 11–17). Whenever ceremonial rites are put in the place of truth and duty they refuse to be silent. Kings, priests, and people by turns receive rebuke at their hands, in everything the true prophet showing himself to be the messenger of God. 'Is not this the fast that I have chosen? to loose the bands of wickedness, to undo the heavy burdens, and to let the oppressed go free, and that ye break every yoke?' (Isa. lviii. 5, 6.)

Further, there runs through the prophecies of these men a long *series of predictions*, which can by no alchemy whatever be interpreted otherwise than as relating to a distant future and to a coming King under whom the world should be happy. Nor is it easy to sever this great monarch from 'the seed of the woman' that was to bruise the head of the serpent; from that descendant of Abraham in whom 'all the nations of the earth' were to be blessed; or from the prophet whom the Lord said unto Moses He would 'raise up of his brethren' like unto Him.

It is this, and the good time connected therewith, which imparts so peculiar a tone and color to all Hebrew prophecy. It is this, as Dean Stanley truly says, that 'gives to the Bible at large that hopeful, victorious, triumphant character which distinguishes it from the morose, querulous, narrow, and desponding spirit of so much false religion ancient and modern. "To one far off Divine event the whole creation moves."' That event—the restoration and happiness of the race under Messiah—is the ever-recurring theme of the Jewish prophets. With a striking prediction of the glorious time when this 'Sun of Righteousness shall rise with healing in His wings' the last of the seers closes at once his own message and the Old Testament.

Need it be said that such predictions if not 'God-breathed' are worse than useless. Professing to be, in the highest sense, Divine, they are either truly so, or else mere outbursts of frantic and fraudulent enthusiasm. If the former, the very words are the words of holy men, speaking 'as they were moved by the Holy Ghost.' If the latter, language has no terms strong enough where-with to denounce such wicked and mischievous impostors.

These prophecies may occasionally be very obscure or very coarse; they may at one time descend to a familiarity that startles us, and at another rise to a sub-limity that is actually overpowering; it may often be exceedingly difficult to separate the voice which refers to its own day, from that which points to a far distant future: but whether clear or dark, whether familiar or sublime, whether referring to the near or to the distant, they stand alone; as compositions unmatched; in beauty without a rival; in purity unapproachable; at once terrible and tender; often mystic and mournful, yet ever redolent of joy and triumph.

The Psalms occupy a position of their own. The Psalter is, as Tholuck says, the book from which 'Piety, whether Jewish or Christian, if genuine, has derived more nourishment than from any other source. In the greater portion of reformed churches they serve as spiritual songs; the Catholic priest daily prays them in his breviary; and, bound with many editions of the New Testament, they form the book of devotion of Protestants. When our Lord instituted the Holy Supper, He sang psalms with His apostles. He testified to His disciples that the traits of His fate were delineated in the Psalms. He referred His opponents to a prophetic psalm as inspired by the Holy Ghost. The extent to which His humiliation and exaltation were, mirror-like, beheld by Him in the Psalms may be illustrated by the fact that, even on the Cross, when expressing the desertion of His soul, He used not His own words, but adopted the language of His typical ancestor."[1]

In this, as in other poetic books, all historic references accord with previously recognised documents. The doctrine or ethics of the Psalms is in exact accordance with that which had preceded them. Herder says, 'There is no attribute, no perfection of God left unexpressed in the simplest and most powerful manner in the Psalms and the Prophets.' Throughout indeed the Old Testament the typical or prefigurative continually appears, 'every pious man who suffered for God's cause

[1] Tholuck, Introd. to Comm. on the Psalms.

under the ancient economy, but triumphed at last, being regarded as a type of what should be fulfilled in Christ; just as the entire sacrificial institutions as well as other phenomena have a like reference.'

But does it follow, if this typical character be admitted, that every book in which it is found must be from first to last inspired of God? We cannot see why this should be assumed. That the Bible, in consequence of the peculiarity of its structure; its mysterious unity; the perpetual murmur of the Infinite which is ever issuing from its pages; in its revelations and in its reticence; in what it says and in what it withholds, is singularly unlike any other book, cannot be disputed. That the Divine breath animates it as a whole; that the Divine mind has controlled its formation, just as the same Divine mind controls and regulates all our affairs; that just as each separate human life, while perfectly free, is yet continually directed by an unseen hand (a thread of the supernatural running through it), so this written embodiment of the life of Humanity growing through the ages, is moulded by One who has made it what it is, is certain. But how this fact should be supposed to carry with it the infallibility of every utterance in the sense of perfect accuracy as to dates and numbers, and absolute approval of every action recorded which is not distinctly disclaimed, it is assuredly difficult to see.

Paley justly observes, 'This is to make Christianity answerable with its life for the circumstantial truth of each separate passage, the genuineness of every book, and for the information, fidelity, and judgment of every writer in it.'

CHAPTER VI.

THE NEW TESTAMENT.

THAT the New Testament opens upon us as *a development* of the Old can scarcely be denied by any honest man. When John the Baptist appears, his message is, 'Repent, for the kingdom of God is at hand.' But no one asks the question, 'What kingdom?' because they fully understood him to be speaking of that which had so long formed the theme of prophetic anticipations. Their views regarding this kingdom might be, as they certainly were, in many respects very defective; for they looked forward to it apart altogether from any moral or spiritual change, and supposed that it would be 'of the earth and earthy.' Nevertheless, it was this gospel of the kingdom, purified indeed from carnality, and connected with the resurrection, that the Apostles were directed to preach, first to the Jew, and then to the Gentile; themselves ever living by faith in the happy expectation of the Redeemer's return, to 'build again the tabernacle of David, and to set it up, that the residue (the rest or remainder) of men might seek after the Lord' (Acts xv. 16–17).

Everywhere in the New Testament, directly or indirectly, the authority of the great lawgiver is recognised. Rites and institutes, circumcision[1] and the sabbath, the passover and the feast of Tabernacles, all commemorate events which, if they never occurred, could not, by any possibility, have become national memorials. The legislation of the land is in great measure that of the wilderness; to honour Moses is to every Jew living in apostolic days the first of duties; to be a child of Abraham the highest of privileges. All this of course supposes that, *at that time*, the Pentateuch was regarded as historic, in the sense of being trustworthy.

Christ Himself distinctly declares that He came not to destroy the law and the prophets, but to fulfil them. He always refers to the Old Testament, and especially to the Pentateuch, as the recognised history of the people. 'Have you never read,' He asks, on one occasion, 'what God said to Moses at the bush?' On another, 'What did Moses command you?' On a third, 'If ye believed Moses ye would believe on Me?' The Flood, the destruction of Sodom and Gomorrah, the falling of the manna, the giving of the law, the elevation of the brazen serpent, are each and all referred to in the New Testament as well-known facts; and Noah, Lot, Jonah, David, Job, Balak, Balaam, and others, are mentioned as historical personages.

[1] '*Circumcision.*'—This, although peculiarly, was *not exclusively* a Jewish rite. It has been found to prevail extensively both in ancient and modern times. It is all but universal among Mohammedans. It belonged to the Jew as to no other people, by its having been appointed or adopted as a sign of the covenant God made with Abraham. It was practised in Egypt, but not during the forty years' sojourn in the wilderness (Josh. v. 5).—Smith's Dictionary.

Stephen, in his defence, recapitulates—although, as we have it, apparently not with perfect accuracy—Jewish history. *Paul*, before Agrippa, insists that he was only teaching the approach of what Moses and the prophets had said should come. In his address to the Jews he reminds them how God called them out of Egypt. In his epistles he refers to the lowly origin of the nation—to 'the hole of the pit' out of which it was digged. He reminds them how the serpent beguiled Eve; how Abraham met Melchisedek; how the law was given to Moses; how they were baptised unto Moses in the cloud and in the sea; how they lusted in the wilderness; how they drank of the rock that was smitten; how, from Abel downwards, the just had lived by faith. *Peter*, in like manner, refers to the Deluge, to the conduct of Lot, and to that of Balaam. *John* speaks of Cain and Abel. *James* of Abraham. *Jude* of Sodom and Gomorrah; while the imagery of the Apocalypse, when narrowly examined, is found to be a curiously wrought piece of Mosaic made up from the older prophets.

The same facts and doctrines everywhere reverberate. The elements which combine in the New Testament are precisely the same as those which characterise the Old. The historic, mingling with the didactic, runs through the Gospels, the Acts, and the Epistles. The predictive is seen in the message of the angel to Mary; in the song of Elizabeth; in the teachings of the Baptist; in the sayings of the Lord, and in that wondrous prophecy which concludes the book. The supernatural appears in miracles without end, wrought, not only by Christ and His apostles, but also by their more immediate converts.

Nor is the morality of the New Testament, as has frequently been asserted, *different* from that of the Old. The ancient commandment is but developed and spiritualised by the Lord Jesus. Nothing is superseded but that which had been ordained or modified in order to meet for a time the peculiar condition of a half civilised people. These ordinances, whether relating to slavery or divorce, to polygamy or concubinage, to judicial retaliation, or to an exclusive nationality, being temporary in character, and borne with for a time in order to avoid greater evils, were to pale and pass away before the higher light brought in by the Redeemer of the world. But it is monstrous to speak, as some do, of the God of Moses as being different or inferior to the God of Isaiah, or of both suffering eclipse before the God and Father of our Lord Jesus Christ.

God is ONE, and His character is One; but man varies with circumstances; and according to those circumstances God deals with him; giving truth, like everything else, only as men are able to bear it, and adapting His enactments to conditions under which higher forms of law would be impracticable, and the attempt to enforce them would only lead to greater mischiefs than legislation could rectify. In this sense the Mosaic dispensation is a different dispensation from that of Christ, its rules, promises, and system being different, though the Author and the End of both dispensations is the same.

Other elements, equally characteristic, might be traced *running through the whole volume*, were it needful to point them out. One in particular may be noticed, viz., the greater favour shown to some above others. We are accustomed to call these preferences instances of Divine sovereignty, simply because they exhibit to us God acting in a way we do not quite understand, and *without giving us any reason* for what He does. The acceptance of Isaac and the rejection (though not without a blessing) of Ishmael; the choice of Jacob over Esau even before birth—though Esau has His blessing too; the selection of Joseph to be ruler over Egypt and the saviour of his family; of Judah, to be eventually the governing tribe; the elevation of Saul; the subsequent choice of David: these, and many other instances, clearly indicate a great purpose running through the ages, in which men are but the instruments of higher power.

In the New Testament, this exercise of Divine sovereignty rises into a doctrine—that of election—and is expounded as such, first by Christ and afterwards by the great apostles of the Gentiles. Need it be observed that, *as a great fact of life*, explain it as we may, the giving to one, and withholding from another meets us at every turn, whether we recognise the hand of God in it or not.

Many other unities might be noticed. If in the Old Testament *as a fact* Cain's offering is rejected because he is hating his brother, in the New *the doctrine* is laid down, man must *first* be reconciled unto his brother, and *then* come and offer his gift. If in the Old Testament Abraham fights bravely for Lot, while Isaac yields his rights rather than contend for them, the counterpart appears in the teaching of the later dispensation, that while the man of God is not to strive, but to overcome evil by good, the soldier may remain in his calling, and the magistrate is not to bear the sword in vain. Under each dispensation the Jacobs with all their sins and weaknesses are regarded as more godly than the Esaus with their rude and manly virtues. *The standard* is the same under both covenants; in each, however, differing very widely from that which any uninspired man would have laid down. *Why* a life of faith should be accepted as covering so many faults—explicable enough to the spiritual man—is an enigma which the world never could, and, on its own principles, never can explain.

Further, of all in the Bible that, properly speaking, *constitutes* the Word of God, that is, the written Word, whether found in the Old Testament or in the New, Christ the *incarnate* Word is at once the centre and the substance. In Him it is all embodied. Around Him all that is written radiates. Some, indeed, have asserted that, in a certain sense, He *typifies* the written Word; that the human element in Scripture is to the Book what human nature was to the Divine Logos; that in the Word written, as in the Word made flesh, the human and the Divine meet without any interference with infallibility. But this can only be affirmed of those portions of the Bible which really *constitute* Divine revelation. In *these*, as in other parts, although in a very different sense, there is *a human element*, but it is one which in no way interferes with infallibility. In Jewish history, however true or important it may be, nothing is to be found corresponding to that union of the Divine and human which was manifested in Christ.

But some will say, This is too general: come to particulars, and tell us plainly whether or no you regard the Gospels as inspired. If so, is it in whole or in part? Further, state distinctly in what light you regard the Acts, the Epistles, and the Apocalypse.

We see no reason to object to such a question, nor do we imagine that, on the principles already laid down, a straightforward reply is to be shunned. Everything in the Gospels that properly constitutes a revelation is unquestionably inspired. The discourses of the Lord must be regarded as *in substance* accurately reported, however words may vary, if we believe that, in accordance with His promise, He supernaturally brought all things that He had said to remembrance, so far as it was needful or desirable that His exact words should be recorded. As a rule, however, it suffices for all practical purposes, that the substance or rather *the real purport* of what was spoken should stand for what was actually said.

The *facts*, or what are stated to be such, are to be received, like all similar statements, on the authority of witnesses, on whose veracity, disinterestedness, and good sense, not a shadow of doubt can rest. Surely, then, we may approach the evangelical narratives with at least *as much respect* as we show to ordinary writers. Surely we are *bound* to peruse them with at least *as much candour* as we are accustomed to exercise when dealing with the productions of any honourable man, whether living, or long since dead. Yet how few sceptics are prepared to do this.

The miracles recorded, if not true narrations of what actually took place, serve only to convict the reporters of being either credulous or fraudulent men, in which case not a word they have written is worthy of a moment's attention from any sensible person. To believe this, however, in the face of statements so calm, unexcited, and well balanced as are those of the Gospels; to associate either weakness or falsehood with men who suffered and died in defence of truth as truth; who lived above all the conventionalities of their day; who had everything to gain by yielding to popular prejudices and to authority in Church and State; who actually lost everything, even life itself, by disregarding the wishes and commands of the rulers: to believe that these men were after all mere charlatans[1] certainly requires an amount of credulity greater than has yet been manifested even by the most zealous upholder of lying legends.

The genealogies inserted by Matthew and Luke, copied in all probability from the public records, *may*, for aught we can tell, be now quite incapable of reconciliation. Matthew, when quoting from the Old Testament, *may* only mean by the phrase 'then was fulfilled' that then again became applicable the words of the prophet. What are sometimes termed 'obscure and incomprehensible prophecies' in the New Testament *may be* mere allusions to passages in the prophetical writings which, by accommodation, illustrate the events narrated. 'The writings of the Jewish prophets,' it has been truly observed by Mr. Hartwell Horne, 'were the *classics* of the later Jews, and in subsequent ages all their writers affected allusions to them.' Interpolations, although of small importance, *may* here or there have crept into the text, and occasional discrepancies

[1] See some observations in the last chapter—'Postscript'—on objections to this dilemma.

can unquestionably be pointed out. But all these things become of little or no consequence, if, recognising the existence of a human element, we keep in mind *the great purpose* for which the Gospels were written. 'These things are written that we may believe that Jesus is the Christ, the Son of God, and that believing we might have life through His name.' He who knows that this was *the end* for which the Gospels were given may well feel assured that the means were adequate; that the Giver would not suffer any error to find place in them which could interfere with the attainment of the end for which they were bestowed.[1]

The developments of doctrine put forth after Pentecost, by Paul and others, whether in the Acts or the Epistles, their advices, commands, and exhortations, rest on the same foundation, and may be subjected to the same conditions as other portions of the New Testament. So far as they *reveal* they are inspired. So far as they are inspired they are infallible. Here, too, however, the human element appears, as when Paul appends to a letter, evidently written under Divine inspiration, directions as to sending his cloak and parchments; or, when he associates with authoritative advices regarding Church matters, the counsel to Timothy, 'Drink no longer water, but use a little wine for thy stomach's sake and thine often infirmities.' And not in these instances only. There is *much* in the Epistles of Paul that is obviously personal, such as expressions of regard for individuals, sometimes inserted on account of the writer and sometimes on behalf of others, which can in

[1] For further observations on the Gospels, see chap. vii. 'The Canon.'

no reasonable sense be regarded as inspired. It is quite otherwise, however, with his authoritative teaching. Here he stands before us as the faithful exponent of the Divine Spirit. The fact that a distinction is, in one instance at least, drawn by Paul himself between speaking by commandment and giving counsel, marks the conscientious integrity of the man, and stamps some other portions not thus separated with an authority which would not, under different circumstances, be so clear.

Nor should *the progressive character* of the teaching of the New Testament—harmonising as it does in this particular too with the Old—be unnoticed. Like its predecessor, it advances step by step as a communication from God. Christ, who is its Alpha and Omega, not only claims to have received from the Father all He taught, He distinctly states that what He had thus received He communicated to His apostles. 'I have given unto them the words which Thou gavest unto Me.'

No statement can be more explicit or more authoritative; for it at one and the same time extends and limits the Divine communication.

It *extends* it to what the apostles should teach after their Lord's departure; and in so doing it assures us that we may rely not only on what He taught them while in the flesh, but on what He communicated to them after He was risen and glorified. It is *an endorsement*, so to speak, of that which was ultimately expanded and developed by them in their epistles to the Churches; it is *an authentication* of that mysterious prediction which concludes the whole.

It *limits* Divine teaching to the men who received what they taught directly from the Lord. It does more; it *limits them* to the expansion of that teaching. Hence the substance of all they taught is involved in the words of Christ. 'All the great doctrinal features of the Epistles are found in germ in separate sayings of Christ. All the main outlines of the Apocalypse are given us in parables and sayings which trace the future history of His kingdom.'

The New Testament thus becomes, like the Old, from first to last *a progressive unity*. But with this difference. '*There* progress is interrupted, often languid, and sometimes so dubious as to seem like retrogression. *Here* it is rapid and unbroken. From the manger of Bethlehem on earth, to the city of God coming down from heaven, the great scheme of things unrolls before us without a check, without a break.'

The Apocalypse, however obscure at present, or however much it may have been abused, is either Divinely inspired in the very highest sense, or, as an eminent sceptic has said, it is 'the most worthless book that was ever placed between covers.' But 'Wisdom is justified of her children.' 'I cannot doubt,' says the present Archbishop of Dublin, 'that a day will come when all the significance of the Apocalypse will be apparent, which hitherto it can scarcely be said to have been. When the great drama is hastening, with even briefer pauses, to its catastrophe; then, in one unlooked for way or another, the veil will be lifted from this wondrous Book, and it will be found strength in the fires, giving songs in the night, songs of joy and deliverance.'

This prophecy, regarded as a prediction of what will

surely one day come to pass, is, like the rest, *bound up* with what has gone before. 'The former Scriptures had revealed the Lord Jesus Christ as the Saviour not only of individual souls, but also of the "body," the Church. The Apocalypse deals with this Church *as a whole*, and presents it as a society, in which man is perfected, and a kingdom, in which God is glorified. The sense of sharing in a corporate existence, and in a history and destinies larger than those which belong to us as individuals, tends to throw the mind forward upon a course of things to come, through which this various history is to run and these glorious destinies to be reached. When present things in a measure disappoint us, we turn more eagerly to the brighter future. Who does not feel in reading the Epistles that some such sense of present disappointment grows upon him, and that such dark shadows are gathering on the scene, that a close like that of the Apocalypse seems to have been demanded?'

'This book,' it has been well said, 'teaches the doctrine of *a blessed consummation*; of its cause, in the death of Christ; of its history and of its nature; of the coming and power of Him whom every eye shall see; of His victory; of the judgment of evil; and of the great and final restoration of all things. Here all the hopes of humanity find at last their realisation—a perfect humanity—perfect, not only individually, but perfect in society. It is the revelation of that which history leads us to despair of; it is the restoration not only of the personal but of the social life; it is the creation not only of the man of God, but of the city of God. Here the revealed course of redemption culminates, and the history of man is closed; and here, in these last chapters of the Bible, the unity of the whole Book is declared by the completion of the design which has been developed in its pages, and by the disclosure of the result to which all preceding steps have tended."[1]

While, however, the recognition of a human element even in the New Testament must be allowed, and may be so without compromising in any degree either the authority of Scripture or the reverence due to it as our guide through life, it is far otherwise with many modern speculations relating thereto. If, as we have been told, the *Jewish element* in the New Testament, that link which connects it with the past, and without which it would be isolated and unmeaning, is a delusion; if we pretend, as some have done, that our Lord, when speaking of His 'kingdom,' was but manifesting the effect of Jewish culture, and was, so far, destitute of spiritual understanding; if we deny the supernatural, and affirm that the miracles were not real; if we are absurd enough to imagine that the writers of the Gospels teach falsehood 'in all purity of intention;' that they narrate as fact mere vague and floating traditions; that they only tell us things 'as they conceived of them;' that the words of the Bible, notwithstanding their falsity, may be regarded as true words, inasmuch as they express 'the conceptions of the times, and the measure of knowledge or of faith to which every one of the writers had in his degree attained:' *then* we had far better abandon the Book at once; for if this be its character, it matters little how soon it may fall into the neglect and contempt it so richly deserves.

[1] Bernard's Bampton Lectures on the Progress of Doctrine in the New Testament. 1864.

Having thus—however rapidly and imperfectly—traced the unity which, amid diversity, distinguishes the various tracts of which the Bible is composed, let us now briefly notice the process by which these treatises were finally brought together and regarded as one book.

CHAPTER VII.

THE CANON.

THE question of the Canon—or what is 'the schedule, so to speak, which contains the books of Scripture'—is a very different one from that of the inspiration of the Bible. 'The object of the Canon,' says Dr. Chalmers, 'is simply to ascertain what are the actual books which should be received into this collection of sacred writings. We may allow a book to be canonical, and yet maintain opinions of all sorts and varieties in regard to its inspiration.' It is important to keep this distinction in view.

The history of the formation of the canon of Scripture is, without doubt, embarrassed by many difficulties. That of the *Old Testament* we accept from the Jews. When or how it was formed is doubtful. Popular opinion assigned to Ezra and the great synagogue the task of collecting and promulgating the Scriptures, as part of their work in organising the Jewish Church. Doubts, however, have been thrown upon this belief. The authority is merely traditional, and a tradition which also regards Ezra as having 'rewritten the whole of the Old Testament from memory, the copies of which had perished by neglect.' Still it is but reasonable to suppose that the people on their return from exile would greatly desire an authoritative collection of their sacred books, and that such should *then* be formed is the more likely from the fact that the assistance of prophets could at this time be obtained, Haggai, Zechariah, and Malachi being cotemporary with Ezra and Nehemiah.[1]

'The history of the canon of the *New Testament* presents a remarkable analogy to that of the Old. The beginnings of both are obscure from the circumstances under which they arose. Both grew silently under the guidance of an inward instinct, rather than by the force of external authority; both were connected with other religious literature by a series of books which claimed a partial and questionable authority; both gained definiteness in times of persecution.'[2] In neither case is there any reason whatever to believe that the work was accomplished under special Divine impulse or guidance. But neither the value nor the trustworthiness of the documents is lessened by the absence of inspired authority in their collection.

Each book must be judged by what it contains. Most emphatically is this true of the Old Testament. As alike canonical, the book of Judges and the prophecies of Isaiah stand side by side, but it by no means thence follows that the contents of each are equally divine. The *former* we accept simply on the authority of Jewish tradition, for of its composition we know nothing. The book evidently embraces an historical period of about 350 years, and therefore, if not given by immediate revelation from heaven, *which there is not the least reason to suppose*, it must have been compiled either from written documents or oral tradition, or from both. In

[1] See Kitto's Cyc., art. 'Ezra.'

[2] Art. 'Canon,' in Dr. Smith's Dict. of the Bible, by the Rev. B. F. Westcott.

any case the *possibility* at least of legendary exaggeration in some of the narratives must be admitted; unless indeed we *assume* (for doing which we have no authority whatever) that God absolutely prevented any such admixture as inconsistent with the end for which the book was written, viz., to show that the Israelites brought upon themselves the calamities under which they suffered by their apostasy and idolatry. The *latter* (the prophecy of Isaiah) carries the evidence of its divinity in its own bosom, and is every way congruous with later revelations.

No such diversity, however, belongs to the books of the New Testament. The four Gospels are, with good reason, regarded as worthy of all acceptation, in the character of authentic and credible documents. But it is by no means easy to *prove* that they are so to the satisfaction of an indifferent observer. The originals, in all probability, perished at a very early period. No autograph of any one of them, so far as appears, was in existence when the canon of the New Testament was completed; nor do we read of anyone who had ever seen them. Further, it can scarcely be disputed that, for many years, the Gospels were not generally known as the productions of the men whose names they bear. It was, without doubt, *long* before the written word occupied any position at all resembling that which it now holds. Nor is this surprising. For, as the Gospel had been at first proclaimed orally, a vivid tradition of this teaching would naturally take the place of any book or books in which it might be embodied. Indeed, for the first hundred and fifty years, the apostolic writings, although in separate circulation, do not seem to have been regarded in any sense as forming one authoritative book. The first catalogue of the books of Holy Scripture drawn up by any public body in the Christian Church, which has come down to us, is that of the Council of Laodicea (A. D. 365). The application of the term Bible to the *collective volume* of the sacred writings cannot be traced above the fourth century. Chrysostom adopts it in his second homily. He adds the word *divine*, or, as we should now express it, 'the Holy Bible."[1]

Yet it can scarcely be doubted that the genuineness of these narratives rests upon evidence better than that which establishes other ancient writings that are received without question. They were all composed during the first century; and it is highly probable that they were all accepted as genuine before the close of the second. Irenæus, who suffered martyrdom A. D. 202, affirms this to have been the case. The differences between the first three Gospels and the fourth seem to find a natural explanation in the fact that John, writing long after the others, purposely abstained from recording anew what was already known on the authority of his predecessors. Whether or no the first three Gospels were compiled from a common original, or whether, to some extent, the writers copied from each other, matters little; each Evangelist gives us his own personal testimony as far as it went; and if they had alike access to documents supposed to be trustworthy, each, by the use he makes of them, gives us his own personal testimony to the accuracy of such fragments. But all this is mere matter of conjecture, and in itself comparatively unimportant.

[1] Kitto's Cycl. of Bib. Lit., edited by Dr. Lindsay Alexander.

Each gospel has its own features, though all conspire to produce an harmonious whole.

The only important question is—How far may the Gospels, as we have them, be relied upon as truthful records? and the answer must, to a great extent, turn upon the reception or rejection of the internal evidence they offer on their own behalf; much of course depending upon our willingness to admit the *possibility* of the supernatural, or our fixed determination, with or without reason, to beg the entire question by refusing to do other than relegate the miraculous to the domain of fiction.

Let not this, however, be regarded as closing the question; for other evidence is not altogether wanting. The literary difficulties which, it is admitted, exist regarding the Gospels, have no place in relation to some at least of St. Paul's Epistles. The genuineness and authenticity of the Epistle to the Romans, and of the two Epistles to the Corinthians, are not disputed; and *in them* we have the most direct and unexceptional evidence to not a few of the statements given us in the Gospels. The Death of Christ and His Resurrection and Ascension, the writer asserts partly no doubt on the testimony of others, but chiefly from what he believed to be a direct communication from the Lord.

If Paul was not a deceiver—and that he was so nobody pretends—the great facts on which the New Testament turns are thoroughly endorsed by a man of the clearest intellect and of the highest character; the most *disinterested* of witnesses; the most richly endowed of all who have professed the Christian faith. Nobody can dispute—whatever may be deduced from the observation—that the Christ of Paul and the Christ of the Gospels are, in all respects, the same; that the miracles of the one correspond to the miracles of the other; and that the teaching, whether ethical or doctrinal, is identical in each. Add to this the consideration, already referred to, which Paley places at the head of so many of his chapters, and it seems difficult to escape the conclusion that these occurrences could scarcely have been better attested.[1]

Yet all this, we are well aware, will go for very little with men in whom spiritual sensibility either slumbers or has never been awakened. There *must* be a correspondence of some kind between the giver and receiver of a testimony; there must be a faculty in exercise for the reception of truth, answering in some degree to the truth presented, or no effect will be produced. If there is nothing *within* a man which, being itself supernatural, witnesses to Divine revelation, it is impossible to produce in such a mind any convictions relating thereto which are worth having.

Two classes of persons commonly manifest a disposition to take advantage, for the furtherance of their own designs, of admissions like those which we have felt compelled to make, viz. the literary sceptic, and the high churchman. The first—the sceptic—tells us that, on our own showing, he is justified in declining to place any confidence in the Gospels, since we allow that he can have no evidence that those now so called are true copies of the original autographs. He argues that, as there is not now extant any manuscript of earlier date

[1] This point has recently been well put by an able writer in the Saturday Review.

than the fourth century, it is impossible to say how far interpolation, subtraction, or addition may have been carried. He affirms that, as we confess we have now no means of knowing by what precise rule the books supposed to be divinely inspired were distinguished from merely human compositions, the supposed authority of the Gospels rests on precisely the same grounds as the infallibility of the pope—that of popular tradition. Finally, he makes the most he can of sundry rash statements found in books 'on the evidences,' and so concludes that he has successfully defended his unbelief. The last—the high churchman—not only to a great extent endorses the sceptic in his conclusions, but magnifies, in every possible way, supposed difficulties, in order to prove thereby the necessity for Church authority.

It is difficult to estimate the amount of mischief that has been done by good men who are bent upon showing that 'the history of the formation of the canon involves little less than the history of the building of the Catholic Church.' Mr. Westcott would not, we suppose, for a single moment place Paul and Ignatius on the same level, and yet he classes them together in telling us that 'the letters of Ignatius complete the history of one feature of Christianity;' that 'the Epistle of St. Paul to the Ephesians, his pastoral epistles, and the epistles of Clement and Ignatius, when taken together, mark an harmonious progression in the development of the idea of a Church.' He allows, indeed, that the productions of these fathers are 'writings of which no exact type can be found in the New Testament,' for 'they exhibit a spirit of order and organization foreign to the first stage of Christian society;' but he does not see in this important admission any reason for the rejection of the letters. Surely it must have occurred to him that since Ignatius was a cotemporary of Pliny the younger, a perusal of that eminent man's unquestioned letter to the Emperor Trajan would alone be sufficient to show how different was the character of early Christianity from that which is presented in the so called Ignatian epistles.

Dr. Irons, in his 'Bible and its Interpreters,' labours to overthrow all confidence in Scripture, except in so far as it is expounded by the Church, and read 'in the light of the creeds, the catechism, and the liturgy.' He regards a 'Book revelation' as 'unreasonable in principle,' forgetting that everything to which man attaches importance he desires to have in writing; that all we know of history comes down to us in books; that books live when tradition dies, and that letters remain unchanged when institutions have altogether lost their original character. And all this he does, simply that in the apparent worthlessness of all other evidence, the Church may lay claim to the absolute submission of men, and teach them to say in every difficulty—'We know this to be so, because the Church has so told us; by her we prove all things, for she has authority in controversies of the faith.'

Surely such writers might with advantage be reminded that blind submission to authority, instead of being faith, renders faith impossible, and that whenever such a claim is thoroughly understood, 'the deep instinct of our spiritual being rises against it; rises as a spiritual instinct of self-preservation against that entire disinheriting of us as God's offspring to which it amounts."[1] Might

[1] M'Leod Campbell: Thoughts on Revelation.

they not well consider whether the very attempt to throw men back upon the authority of 'fathers' whose writings have themselves reached us in most questionable shapes, and to make out that, if we accept the Gospels at all, it must be in reliance on the judgment or supposed semi-inspiration of turbulent assemblies of bishops, such as were those so graphically depicted by Dean Stanley in his lectures on the Eastern Church—men who but too often exhibited as much ignorance as credulity; might they not, indeed, well consider whether the very attempt to do this is not to betray the cause of the Bible, in order to exalt the pretensions of the Church?

But it may be replied, Is not this after all the truth of the matter? Is it not universally admitted that the councils of Laodicea and Carthage are our authorities for the New Testament canon? To a certain extent it undoubtedly is so; but only in so far as these assemblies may be regarded trustworthy witnesses to the fact that, at a very early period, given documents were *commonly received* as genuine. The all-important inquiry is, not what the councils decided, but what reasons *Christians* had, in that day, for accepting certain books and rejecting others. And the true answer will probably be found partly in traditions, which were then comparatively fresh; and partly in that 'witness of the Spirit' to the truths embodied in the accepted books, which has been in all ages, and still is, the highest evidence to their canonicity.

The apostle John, it is admitted, lived upwards of thirty years after the production of every apostolic writing, except his own apocalypse. It is surely, then, not unreasonable to suppose that he was in possession, before his death, of all inspired productions, or that he was instructed as to which of them were intended for the permanent guidance of the Church. We may naturally wonder that, under such circumstances, the apostle did not furnish for publication a formal and complete list of books which ought to be accepted; but we can gather nothing from the omission to do so beyond this, that so far as we can see, it was not on the whole deemed desirable that the thing should be done. The acquisition of truth is, in all its stages and relations, *probationary;* and no unimportant element in that probation is the pains we take to collect evidence, and the mode in which we deal with it when obtained.

Polycarp, who was a disciple of John, would, one would think, be sure to receive from his aged teacher such information as would enable him to decide what writings then in circulation were or were not authoritative; and Irenæus, who heard Polycarp preach, would, in all probability, obtain from the martyr or from his immediate friends information so likely to be regulative of his teaching. From the time of Irenæus it is generally admitted that the New Testament was composed 'essentially of the same books as we receive at present, and that they were regarded with the same reverence as is now shown to them.'

If this be true, and there is no reason to doubt its substantial accuracy, all that the councils would have to do would be to verify these things and to act upon them. This was done; but in doing it, and in publishing a catalogue of the books then held to be inspired, these assemblies simply bore witness to the general belief of the existing churches that such, and such only, ought to be accepted. This is evident from the fact that some books were received into the canon later than others, use and enquiry combining to give them in course of time their proper place. Beyond this the councils could do nothing; for the men who there met could not personally know more about the matter than we do. Like Christians of the present day, they were not insensible to the internal evidence they found in favour of the books they accepted, or to their accordance with the instincts of the new nature. But in this particular they were but on a level with ourselves, as we again are, in this respect, on a level with those who spiritually lived on Scripture, long before its books were catalogued or any council had decided on the canon.

Granting, then, as we readily may, that in the very earliest controversies about disputed readings, we have no evidence of any appeal having been made to apostolic originals; granting that 'the full value of the Divine gift' was not at first known, since 'in the first age the written word of the apostles occupied no authoritative position above their spoken word, or the vivid memory of their personal teaching;' admitting that pretended gospels were, at one time, almost countless in number, we are stiil by no means driven either to renounce the authority of Scripture or to fall back upon the Church.

It is easy to say, How can I accept the Gospels we have, unless I know *the grounds* on which they were accepted and other writings of a similar character rejected? But it is not sensible to do so. We do not speak thus regarding such pretended gospels as are yet extant. Why do we not ourselves accept the so called

'Apocryphal New Testament,' with its gospel of the infancy, its various epistles, its shepherd of Hermas, and such like productions? Is any other reply needful than this—They condemn themselves? No reasonable person imagines for a moment that any one of these writings can compete with those that are canonical. There is scarcely room for a doubt or a question either as to their authority or their value. Why may we not then suppose that this was precisely the case with the early churches? These judges give no reasons for their decisions, simply because they never had a question regarding the claims of other documents which even admitted of serious discussion. The genuine Gospels carry their own evidence with them: they are seen to be Divine by their own light. But this, of course, implies that true Christians have, by virtue of their Christianity, a gift of spiritual insight, in the light of which they can separate the true from the false.

It is not surprising that many should be unprepared to admit this; that they should demand objective evidence; that they should be altogether unable to estimate the force of that which is purely subjective; that having themselves never received anything which the Gospels reveal *into their hearts*, they should refuse to do more than stand outside, and coolly weigh what is to be said in favour of the authenticity and inspiration of Scripture in scales of their own making, and apart altogether from any considerations that are moral and spiritual. While this is the case, such persons must remain unsatisfied. The Bible always supposes the existence in the man to whom it speaks of a spiritual faculty having affinity with its revelations; and this being the case, and ordained of God, it is vain to offer evidence in favour either of the miracles of the New Testament or of the authority of the Gospels to persons who are as yet quite unprepared to estimate that Divine love and condescension which underlies all. 'My sheep,' says Christ, 'know My voice.' Only in this way is it given to men, as Mr. Tennyson says,

> To feel, although no tongue can prove
> That every cloud that spreads above
> And veileth love, itself is love.

To the man who accepts the Bible because he recognises in it the Divine voice, the human authorship becomes a matter of small importance. The Gospels would occupy precisely the same place in the estimation of such a man as they now do, whatever amount of doubt might be thrown on their literary composition. It is certainly pleasant to feel assured that the Epistle to the Romans, for instance, was written by Paul, but it would scarcely be less valued if, like the Epistle to the Hebrews, its authorship were uncertain. To say, therefore, that evidence of the authorship is essential to confidence in the books; to affirm that if the Bible is not infallibly accurate in every particular, it does not differ from other writings; to insist that it ought not to be received as a Divine revelation unless separate proof for the infallibility of each distinct portion can be presented; to pretend that if an erroneous statement can be discoverep in any part of the volume the worthlessness of the whole is demonstrated: is simply to affirm that under no conditions whatever shall its authority be acknowledged; that any truth it may contain, if accepted at all, must be accepted only because it is capable of being proved true by other means; that nothing is to be received as true merely because it is contained in the Bible.

Yet the Book *lives.* And in spite of the admission that authority, tradition, and literary evidence, all go, more or less, to form or to build up our faith in it, it remains true that, apart from all these things, learned and ignorant alike 'have hung over this Book as with a strange fascination, ever since it was known to be put together as a whole;' some dreading it, as if it were an enemy, others loving it as the dearest and best of friends; *both* not unfrequently being compelled to exclaim, 'It tells me all things that ever I did. Is it not from God?' This is, probably, what Coleridge means when he says, 'The Bible *finds me* in a way no other book does. I do not so much find it, as I am found of it.'

How much more satisfactory, say some men, it is to rest our faith upon God than upon documents! Doubtless it is so; but before such a dictum can be accepted, in the sense which these objectors put upon it, we must be informed where and how any true knowledge of God is to be obtained, if the documents in question are to be either rejected or ignored? Let us, therefore, instead of yielding to dissatisfaction with *the mode* in which God has been pleased to reveal Himself, now apply that which has been advanced to what are generally regarded as difficulties in Scripture.

CHAPTER VIII.

DIFFICULTIES IN THE BIBLE.

Difficulties in Scripture are of various kinds; some pertaining to the letter, and others to the spirit or sentiment expressed or implied. Those in the Pentateuch which are supposed to involve statements that are unscientific, or otherwise inaccurate, may surely be disposed of by considerations already advanced, viz., that Scripture was not written for the men of the nineteenth century alone, but for persons altogether unacquainted with our modern science; that some things recorded probably involve to a limited extent figures of speech; that infallibility in regard to minor matters is nowhere claimed for the narratives in question.

It is difficult to see how *any* official record or narrative of well-known facts can be regarded as written under Divine inspiration, without lowering the term to an extent that altogether changes its signification; unless indeed it is intended to imply thereby that the writer has been miraculously preserved from error, and also been enabled to correct any mistakes he may find in the documents he copies, or from which he quotes. This is of course to assert that Jewish history, in all its most minute particulars is, so far as it is given in Scripture, equivalent to a directly God-breathed communication, for nothing else can be infallible.

Those who hold to this view are, however, obliged to allow that the miracle they assert has not been prolonged through the ages, by the supernatural preservation of the Book thus composed from all the accidents to which written records, however carefully guarded, become in course of time liable. If the Book had been thus preserved, it is impossible that errors such as those already referred to[1] could have been found in it. But if, as is evident, this has not been done; if it was not needful, in order that the purposes of God should be accomplished, that a perpetual miracle should be wrought for the preservation of the document, it is hard to see that a miracle should have been either wrought or required in order to enable honest and truth-loving men who lived in the fear of God, to write with adequate accuracy the well-known history of their people. All the probabilities, therefore, if we bear in mind the established fact that God never works a miracle needlessly, are in favour of the supposition that no such miracle was wrought; in which case errors, where they exist, must be attributed either to the original imperfection of the writers, or to the carelessness or dishonesty of later transcribers.

Difficulties, however, remain which cannot thus be disposed of. These arise—

1. From the observation that certain transactions—attributed to judges or other distinguished personages—which everyone would now admit to be immoral, are, in Scripture, not only recorded without disapprobation, but sometimes, as in the cases of Deborah and David, made the subject of song and thanksgiving. The actions

[1] Chap. ii. 'The Extent of the Claim,' pp. 18, 19.

of Jael, of Rahab, of Ehud, and of Samson are of this character.

2. That certain practices, such as the putting to death of the Canaanites, slavery, and polygamy—the latter distinctly or implicitly condemned by Christ and His apostles—are both tolerated and legislated for; while other laws, such as those relating to witchcraft, indicate nothing better than superstitious ignorance.

3. That the phrases, 'Thus saith the Lord,' or 'The Lord said,' are sometimes used under circumstances that seem to involve the Divine Being in acts which stand in direct contradiction to His character as revealed to us in Christ. The hanging of Saul's seven sons before the Lord is a striking instance of this kind.

4. That some of the supposed miracles of the Old Testament were wrought under circumstances which seem to be, so far as we are able to form any judgment on the subject, altogether unworthy of the Creator and so far out of harmony with other displays of supernatural power.

5. That, even in the New Testament, doctrines are by many supposed to be taught—such for instance as that of election and the eternal sensitive torment of unbelievers—which are inconsistent with declarations found elsewhere regarding God's love to His creatures and His pitifulness to their infirmities; while other doctrines, like that of the Trinity, appear to contradict the Divine Unity.

6. That the general unintelligibility of Scripture, which is manifested in incessant disputes and divisions *as to what the Book says*, forbids the belief that it is a message from God to man; since, if it had been, what-

ever peculiarities might have distinguished it, the document itself would at least have been plain and unmistakeable.

To each of these points it is essential that attention should be paid, if stumbling-blocks are to be removed out of the way of honest and enquiring minds. We take them up therefore in order; and in so doing observe—

1. That the treachery of Jael, the deceit of Rahab, the assassination of Eglon by Ehud, and the savagery of Samson, are simply recorded as historical facts. The song of Deborah by no means carries with it any evidence that what Jael did had the Divine approval. True, the poet who praises her was a prophetess, and one raised up to judge Israel in a time of peculiar depression; but she was not on that account infallible either in her conduct or utterances. If Peter, the first of apostles, had to be withstood, because even in seeking to promote the faith of Christ he was to be blamed; if John, in zeal for his Master's honour did, on one occasion at least, speak not knowing what spirit he was of, why should we fear to admit that Deborah, on this particular occasion, like David in some of his imprecatory psalms, manifests patriotism rather than piety, and, carried away by natural enthusiasm, prophesies in a spirit which is not Divine?[1]

'Most people,' says an able writer,[2] 'have felt some perplexity at the commendation which the author of the Epistle to the Hebrews bestows on such characters as those of Samson and Jephthah, of Gideon and of Barak. Certainly these men are not such as we should have

[1] See Vaughan's Way to Rest, sect. iv. pp. 125, 126.

[2] Art. on Dean Stanley's Jewish History, in Fraser's Magazine.

expected to find held up as patterns, enrolled in such a band of faithful servants of God as Abraham, Isaac, Moses, and Samuel: it scarcely accords with our theories of inspiration to read of the Spirit of the Lord descending upon such a one as Samson with his vices and his weaknesses, and prompting him to his wild acts of vengeance on his own false friends and his country's enemies; arming Gideon for the punishment of Succoth and Peniel; or Jephthah for the wholesale slaughter of the Ephraimites. Yet so speaks the sacred narrative, and the inspired commentator is not afraid to acknowledge these fierce patriots as lights of God's chosen people, as those who '*by faith* subdued kingdoms, obtained promises, waxed valiant in fight, turned to flight the armies of the aliens.' It is *for their faith* they are commended, and it may be truly said of them that the imperfection of their characters, the disorder of their times, set forth the more clearly the one redeeming element of trust in God that lurked in each of them, and through them kept alive the national existence. These deeds must surely be viewed by the light of their own times and their own race; they must be judged according to their own code of morals, not by that which Christianity has rendered as it were elementary to us. Like other Orientals, they were profoundly indifferent as to the choice of means when they had succeeded in persuading themselves that the end to be obtained was the will of God.'

Is it not possible, we may add, as Dean Stanley has suggested, that the book in which these strange things occur—that of the Judges—has been given to us 'with the express view of enforcing upon us the necessity which we are sometimes anxious to evade, of recognising the human, national, let us even add, barbarian element which plays its part in the sacred history?'

Those who hold that God directed the Judges in all that they did as rulers of the people, are of course driven to assume that Jehovah commanded, or distinctly approved every one of the acts referred to, and then rightly arguing that no deed *can* be immoral which God justifies, they maintain all these acts to be right. This course would be very reverential and praiseworthy were it *quite certain* that what they assume is true. But what if it should not be? Surely the strongest evidence ought to be forthcoming that God *did* actually command these things to be done, and that the book in which they are recorded was God-breathed, *before* we are required to admit that the Divine Being ever did or ever will command His children to do anything that He has Himself taught them to be wrong. Yet this is just the very evidence that is wanting.

2. The difficulties supposed to arise out of the massacre of the Canaanites and the permission of slavery have already been dealt with.[1] It is not therefore necessary to revert to them again. The permission of an evil like polygamy, under the circumstances then prevailing, is not so very difficult to account for, if it be recollected that in all His dealings with the children of Israel the Lord never disregarded the customs of the time in which His people lived, or ever set aside any surrounding influence which was not morally destructive to them. The laws given from time to time were not always ordained because they were abstractly the best,

[1] See Correspondence, 'Reply to the Doubter,' pp. 32, 33.

but as being the best *they* under the circumstances could bear. Some of them were avowedly temporary, and some—as the Sabbatic year for instance—appear to have been rarely if ever carried out. In the wilderness, whére but little flesh was eaten, they were forbidden to slay any animal for food except at the door of the Tabernacle (Levit. xvii. 1–7). In Palestine, or rather just before they entered it, this law was superseded by a distinct permission to kill and eat flesh anywhere (Deut. xii. 15–27). Polygamy and concubinage seem to have been allowed only to prevent greater evils, just as slavery, which existed universally, was, as we have seen, in the interests of humanity, modified in Israel to an extent unknown anywhere else.

Of the sorcery and witchcraft referred to in various parts of Scripture we know little or nothing beyond the fact that its practice was a crime punishable by death. *That*, however, as Mr. De Quincey has well observed, 'does not argue any Scriptural recognition of witchcraft as a possible offence. An *imaginary* crime may imply a criminal intention that is *not* imaginary; but also—which much more directly concerns the interests of a state—a criminal purpose that rests upon a mere delusion may work by means that are felonious for ends that are fatal. At this moment we, the English people, have laws, and severe ones, against witchcraft, viz. in the West Indies; and indispensable it is that we should. The Obeah man from Africa can do no mischief to one of *us*; the proud and enlightened white man despises his arts; and for *him*, therefore, these arts have no existence, for they work only through strong preconceptions of their reality, and through trembling faith in their efficacy. But by that very agency they are all-sufficient for the ruin of the poor credulous negro, and he has perished by a languishing decay thousands of times, under the knowledge that *Obi* had been set for him. Justly, therefore, do our colonial courts punish the Obeah sorcerer, who, though an impostor, is not the less a murderer.'

'Now, the Hebrew witchcraft was probably even worse than this; equally resting on delusions, it nevertheless equally worked for unlawful ends, and it worked through idolatrous agencies, for all the spells, the rites, the invocations, were pagan. The witchcraft of Judea, therefore, must have kept up that connection with idolatry which it was the unceasing effort of the Hebrew polity to exterminate from the land.' [1] It must, however, be admitted that there is a mystery about all the Satanic action referred to in the Bible, which we are as yet unable to solve. That a belief in sorcery prevailed among the Jews even in our Lord's time is evident from the Pharisees accusing Jesus of working His miracles by the power of Beelzebub; and the very little we ourselves know about the invisible world, either of angels or demons, may well restrain us from hasty dogmatism on such a subject.

The folly and sin of our forefathers in burning supposed witches consisted not in the mere persuasion—however destitute of reason—that sorcery was *possible*, but in their superstitious and selfish dread of evil powers; their silly credulity; and their atrocious cruelty towards those whom they ought to have pitied and

[1] De Quincey's Miscellanies, vol. viii.

assisted. In order to disbelieve in witchcraft, it is not necessary to become a Sadducee.

3. The question whether all that is attributed to God in the Old Testament can confidently be asserted to have been done by Him, is one that will be answered in the affirmative or otherwise, according as we admit or refuse to admit *the possibility* of interpolation; according to the interpretation we put upon the words 'Thus saith the Lord;'[1] according as we hold to, or abandon, the plenary inspiration, and consequent infallibility of every statement made in the Bible. It is surely, to say the least of it, very *improbable* that when Saul in his pride and rashness had on one occasion adjured the people, saying, 'Cursed be the man that eateth any food until the evening that I may be avenged on mine enemies,' the Lord should not only withhold an answer from the priest because Jonathan had ignorantly and therefore innocently disobeyed, but *first* signify by the lot that Jonathan should die for the sin, and *then* suffer the people, in indignant defiance of the decision, to rescue him. Yet so it stands (1 Sam. xiv.), and, so standing, all but proclaims aloud that in some part of the narrative there is error.

It is, as we have already said, perhaps impossible for us to know how far *a liability* to mistake or to evade a Divine communication, whether given by voice or vision, was incurred by him who received it. But it may safely be asserted that all the probabilities are, that not only to the ancient prophet, but to everyone who received such intimations, a Divine message was always *probationary*; and this in the sense that *all action*,

[1] See Correspondence, 'Reply to the Doubter,' pp. 35–39.

whether on the mind or heart of man by the Spirit of God, is still probationary—that is to say, capable of being misunderstood, resisted, or absolutely rejected by a proud or rebellious spirit. Faith and humility must surely have found as much room for exercise *then* as they now do; and if so, only by an unction from above was the Divine message or warning understood or regarded.

Further, it must be borne in mind, that among the Israelites, phrases implying a direct appeal to heaven were commonly used when no such communications really took place. Seeking an ordinary decision at law is in this way called enquiring of God. Moses says (Exod. xviii. 15), 'The people come unto me *to enquire of God*.' The following verse explains to us in what sense this phrase was used, for he adds, 'I judge between one and another, and I do make them know the statutes of God and His laws.' Moses, as a wise legislator and administrator, was undoubtedly in these cases *the representative* of God; but to assume that because this was the case every separate decision of his was infallible, or that God, so to speak, was responsible for all His servant did, is surely but an extravagance.

That Judea was governed theocratically, in a sense altogether peculiar and exceptional, cannot reasonably be doubted if Israelitish history be accepted as true. The heathen nations around them might, as they did, claim, like the Jew, to unite the secular and the religious in their government; they might boast, as they sometimes were accustomed to do, of the power of their gods, and of their intervention on their behalf; they might resort to omens and auguries as a means of ascertaining the will of superior divinities; but to Judea alone belonged *the reality* of which all these things were but deceptive shadows. For them as a nation, and on behalf of their national interests, God did at times unquestionably interfere, although, strange as it must seem to us, the most marked interference seems often to have had little or no corresponding effect on the minds of the people. 'The great mass of them went about their daily occupations with probably neither more nor less reference to the Divine Being than the masses of the English people do at this day.' The more religious few were then, as they ever have been, whether among Jews or Gentiles, a small minority.

Bearing in mind these conditions—liability to error arising from moral causes, on the part of the recipient, and *the possibility* of interpolation—we may, I think, *safely and without irreverence*, deny the authority of all statements which assert that God *ever did* command any act which is obviously alien to His character as revealed in Christ; and, further, that this may be done without the slightest danger of thereby rejecting any portion of inspired Scripture.

The sacrifice of Saul's seven sons (2 Sam. xxi. 8) certainly appears to be so contrary to all that God has made known of Himself elsewhere, that it may well be questioned whether this portion of the narrative is not altogether an interpolation. The story, as it stands, asserts that a three years' famine having distressed the land, David enquired of the Lord in order to ascertain the reason of so terrible a punishment; that the Lord answered him by stating that it was a judicial infliction on account of Saul having at some period or other of his history, for we know not when, in his zeal for Israel, sought to slay the Gibeonites (Josh. ix. 3–27). In order to placate the Divine anger on account of this *evil design* on the part of the dead monarch, the seven sons of Saul are said to have been *hung up unto the Lord* in Gibeah, after which God was entreated for the land.

The question is, not so much whether this act, whatever may be its character, actually took place, as whether God did actually command or approve of it.[1] That it is utterly unlike everything else recorded of Jehovah is clear. Which course, then, is most reverent? To *assume* its truth, as divines generally do, and then confess our inability to judge of its rectitude—David having sworn to Saul that when he reached the kingdom he would not cut off his seed (1 Sam. xxiv. 20–22)—*or* to question whether it may not be an interpolation? Of course we cannot *prove* that it is so; but inasmuch as no one doubts that some few passages of the New Testament have been thus wrongfully introduced, and therefore form no part of Scripture, it is at least *possible* that such *may* have been the case with some portions of the Old.

[1] The Rev. David Jas. Vaughan, in a sermon on 'The Moral Difficulties of the Bible,' suggests, regarding this transaction, that David was probably deceived by the priest who answered *as from the Lord.* 'It is for Saul, and for his bloody house, because he slew the Gibeonites.' That suspicion, he says, 'is increased when we remember that the priest, to whom David must have applied, would be that Abiathar, who alone had escaped from the bloody massacre of the priests at Nob, which Saul in a fit of brutal passion had commanded, and who would be sure to entertain feelings of the deepest hatred, and a truly Oriental thirst for revenge against Saul and his house.'

That it is justifiable *occasionally* to resort to conjecture in Old Testament criticism can scarcely be denied. Dr. Davidson's remarks on this head are both moderate and judicious. 'The step is,' he says, 'sometimes *unavoidable*. In consequence of the paucity and youth of all Hebrew manuscripts, the uncritical state in which the oldest and best versions are found, and the comparative poverty of external evidence as a whole, added to the great extent of the Old Testament books, and the remote times from which they have been handed down, the necessity of applying critical conjecture in the case of the Old Testament becomes apparent. Yet it should be used sparingly. The only rule respecting its application is, when a pressing necessity arises let it be adopted.' And surely no necessity can be greater than that which presents itself when anything is attributed to God that is contrary to the revelation He has made of Himself in other parts of the written Word. Such is the case before us.

Mr. Horne, indeed, tells us, in the 'Critical Introduction,' that the corruption of the Old Testament by the Jews was *morally impossible*.[1] But no assertion can be more extravagant. That it has been subjected to at least the same risks as the New Testament cannot be doubted, and if interpolation can be *proved* to have taken place in but a single instance in the one, it is by no means improbable that it may have been effected in the other. And this may be admitted without at all either denying or undervaluing the remarkable care which has been taken of the books as a whole, or their providential preservation by God.

[1] Crit. Int., 3rd edition, vol. i. p. 117.

'How often the separate books were transcribed, or with what degree of correctness, it is impossible to tell. We cannot suppose that the Old Testament writings were perfectly free from alterations in the earliest times. It is probable that they had been deteriorated even in the interval between their origin and the completion of the canon. All analogy confirms this supposition.' It is granted that 'the Palestinian Jews were very scrupulous in guarding the text from innovation; although it is impossible that they could have preserved it from *all* corruption.' It seems impossible to doubt that *opportunities* for interpolation would easily enough be found between the times of Ezra and the destruction of Jerusalem, and it is matter for thankfulness that 'the operations of sacred criticism have proved that there is *no material corruption* in the Divine records; that all doctrines and duties remain unaffected by its investigations; and that during the lapse of so many centuries, the Holy Scriptures have been preserved in a surprising degree of purity.'[1]

The passage now under notice (2 Sam. xxi. 8) has every appearance of being interpolated for the purpose of justifying the more zealous adherents of David in having compassed the death of all claimants to his throne who were likely to be troublesome, a practice which then universally prevailed. Be this as it may, the transaction described is certainly out of harmony with other parts of Divine revelation, and the act, if it ever took place, was a direct violation of the oath by which David had pledged himself to Saul to preserve his children. The incident, as it stands, is quite un-

[1] Kitto's Bib. Cycl. art. 'Biblical Criticism.'

connected with any other part of Scripture, and its withdrawal does not affect any fact or doctrine elsewhere stated. No one is bound to believe that, under the Old Testament dispensation, God either commanded or approved any transaction the moral character of which cannot be defended. Treachery, falsehood, or the indulgence of a revengeful spirit in any form, are not to be regarded as approved by God because they may be narrated without disapprobation by the historian. That they could be, would never have entered the mind of any man, but for the supposed necessity of sustaining the plenary inspiration of every part of the Bible.

The extermination of the Midianites, which has already been noticed in connection with other remarks on the massacre of the Canaanites,[1] appears at first sight to have been marked by a peculiarly disgusting feature, the sparing of the female children and virgins, since it is commonly assumed by objectors that these were reserved for prostitution. Very little reflection, however, will suffice to show that this was not the case. 'The law prohibited an Israelite even from marrying a captive without delays and previous formalities; and if he afterwards divorced her, he was bound to set her at liberty because he had humbled her (Deut. xxi. 10–14). They were allowed to retain these Midianitish captives *only* as slaves, educating them, when they did their duty, in their families, and employing them as domestics, because being yet uncorrupted they could do so without moral danger.

The conduct of David towards the Ammonites (2 Sam. xii. 31) has been also represented as an act of

[1] See Correspondence, 'Reply to the Doubter,' p. 37.

diabolic cruelty, since he is said to have 'put them under saws, and under harrows of iron, and under axes of iron, and made them pass through the brick-kiln.' This charge vanishes when it is seen that the Hebrew word translated 'under,' means also 'to.' The statement, properly rendered, is that he employed them as slaves in sawing wood, working harrows (or perhaps iron mines), and in making bricks.

The slaughter of the Amalekites, on the supposition that it was commanded by God,[1] has been said to justify, or at least to furnish an apology for, religious persecution, since it seems to teach that the destruction by man of those who are regarded as the enemies of God, is pleasing in the Divine sight. But it really inculcates no such lesson; for neither Moses nor Joshua, nor indeed any person mentioned with approbation in Scripture, ever made war on any nation on this ground, beyond the borders of the promised land. They had no commission to overthrow idolatry by the sword; no command to destroy idolaters as such out of their own land, and *they never attempted to do it.* The particular tribes inhabiting Palestine who refused to depart, and resisted in battle the armies of Israel, were indeed so dealt with, but *not the heathen generally.* On the contrary, the prophets plead their cause along with that of the widow and the fatherless, and one of them at least looks forward with joy to the time when they shall be in all respects equal with Israel (Ezek. xlvii. 22). What, indeed, can be more touching than the declaration that the Lord loveth the stranger (the heathen) in giving him food and raiment? 'Love ye therefore,'

[1] See Correspondence, 'Reply to the Doubter,' pp. 38, 39..

He says, 'the stranger: for ye were strangers in the land of Egypt' (Deut. x. 19).

4. The fact that certain miracles are recorded in the Old Testament of a character not in harmony with the general principles that characterize the exercise of superhuman power in other cases, again suggests the *possibility* of interpolation. We say *certain* miracles, because, as a rule, the miraculous in the Old Testament is marked by precisely the same features as in the New. These features are benevolence, dignity, and congruity with all that is revealed of the character of God. There is nothing theatrical about them, no mere wonder-working, nothing aimless and objectless, nothing monstrous or prodigious. In each and all of them we see 'the supernatural standing in relation to the Infinite,' and we are awed rather than startled as we gaze. But it can scarcely be said that this is true of *all* the miracles recorded in Jewish history. There are *exceptional* cases, and in relation to these some doubt may well be entertained.

As we have just observed, the direct interferences of God, whatever their object, whether visible or invisible, whether accomplished through the agency of the elements, or by a power which left no sign, are all marked be a majesty and dignity which stamps them as Divine. For whatever we may say or think as to what would be really involved in the shadow going back on the sundial of Ahaz; however ignorant we are as to whether the overthrow of the walls of Jericho was or was not occasioned by the agency of an earthquake; whether or no the destruction of the Assyrian army was effected by means of a deadly simoom, or literally by an angel of

God; whether the speaking serpent in Eden was an actual animal or but the embodiment of Satan; whether the voice of the ass rebuking Balaam was actual speech or only an utterance subjective to the prophet, matters little, so long as we recognise in these things the supernatural interference of the Creator, and regard them as equally supernatural with the appearance of the pillar of cloud and of fire, the descent of God on Mount Sinai, and the Resurrection of the Redeemer.

Most of us have, no doubt, always thought of the passage of the Red Sea as having been effected calmly, the waters quietly parting as Moses waved the rod. Yet our faith is not endangered when we come to perceive that Dean Stanley is, in all probability, right, in supposing that it took place amid a hurricane of wind; the sea roaring as it was driven back, and the darkness being lit up by streams of lightning. By taking this view, we come to understand better than we otherwise should the sublime words of David when he says, 'The waters saw Thee, O God, the waters saw Thee; they were afraid: the depths also were troubled. The voice of Thy thunder was in the heaven: the lightnings lightened the world: the earth trembled and shook. Thy way is in the sea, and Thy path in the great waters, and Thy footsteps are not known. Thou leddest thy people like a flock by the hand of Moses and Aaron' (Ps. lxxvii. 18–20).

The real difficulty connected with *some* of the miracles recorded in the Old Testament is not their supposed supernatural character, but the circumstances under which they are said to have been wrought. The lofty command of Joshua, uttered amid the excitement of battle, and in the sight of Israel, 'Sun stand thou still upon Gibeon; and thou, Moon, in the valley of Ajalon,' followed as it is by the declaration that 'the sun stood still, and hasted not to go down *about a whole day*,' is of this character, especially when the authority for the statement is said to be the Book of Jasher, of which we know nothing (Josh. x. 13). The difficulty is not in the unscientific character of the language, for that might be colloquial; nor yet in any miraculous prolongation of light if God so willed it, but in the tone of the whole transaction.

Again, certain miracles said to have been wrought by Elisha, such as the healing of the waters of Jericho, *at the request of the men of the city*, so that dearth or barrenness should not be there any more (2 Kings ii. 19–22); the cursing of those who mocked him, and the consequent destruction of forty-two young men (not 'little children') by two she-bears (2 Kings ii. 23–4); the making iron to swim in order that one of the sons of the prophets might secure a borrowed axe (2 Kings vi. 5); and the return to life of a man accidentally cast into the prophet's sepulchre when the corpse touched Elisha's bones (2 Kings xiii. 21), have all of them a very apocryphal appearance; inasmuch as, in each instance, they are wrought for purposes which—reverently speaking and in the light of Scripture alone—seem to us to be unworthy of Divine interference. In one case the miracle seems to be wrought merely to meet the wishes of men apparently seeking only their own advantage; in another to carry out what certainly looks like vindictive revenge for personal insult; in a third, to save the cost of a small purchase; and in the last apparently for no object whatever beyond mere wonder-working.

Now, the question is, *on what principle* can these stories about Elisha be rejected, if the second book of Kings, in which they are found, is to be retained, and if other statements contained therein regarding the same prophet are to be believed? The answer seems to be, Either by accepting the second book of Kings in its true character—that of an historical record, but supposing it to have been composed by men who were liable to accept floating traditions without sufficient discrimination—*or* that the work has been somewhat with at a later period. The latter seems to be far the more probable explanation. If any evidence can be produced to show that the second book of Kings was, as a matter of fact, written by men who were miraculously preserved from error, and further that no interpolation can by possibility have taken place, *then* of course we are bound to accept all that is contained therein, and to believe that—account for it as we may—the great principles which dignify and sustain the miracles of our Lord and His apostles were not adhered to under the Old Testament dispensation.

But surely we ought not to come to such a conclusion either hastily or on insufficient grounds. The *test*, be it remembered, by which these stories are to be tried is *the Word of God itself*, not mere human opinion; the ground of rejection is precisely the same as that on which the story of Tobit and the fish, and of Bel and the Dragon were originally pronounced untrustworthy. Nothing, therefore, can be more unwarranted than the popular cry—too often encouraged by those who ought to know better—that any exercise of the verifying faculty in the present day *must* end in each man's accepting or rejecting just as much of Scripture as may suit him.

Such an assertion is unwarrantable: (1) Because, as we have already said, the test applied is not human but Divine. (2) Because, being such, its application belongs only to those whose spirits have by Divine grace been more or less brought into harmony with the Divine Will. (3) Because it is *the* principle—almost the only ruling principle—on which any settlement of the canon has ever proceeded. At the very earliest period tradition no doubt had great weight, but as this weakened by lapse of time the spiritual discernment of the Churches became paramount. (4) Because it is, in all respects, more to be depended upon than any mere comparison of manuscripts would be, were they in existence. We say *mere* comparison, because the *rejection*, for instance, of the text known as 'the three heavenly witnesses,' while partially justified by its absence from early manuscripts, is far more conclusively supported by its own character. On the other hand, the *retention* of the narrative of the woman taken in adultery, although wanting in so many copies, is not only justified by internal evidence, but also by the far greater probability that such a narrative should have been excluded, as dangerous, at a time when inflated and exaggerated notions about virginity were prevalent, than that it should have been interpolated under any circumstances whatever.

In relation to the New Testament there is probably but one miracle that is fairly questionable—that of the supposed periodical descent of an angel into the pool of Bethesda. And this is rejected by believing critics on precisely the same grounds as those that have been stated—its want of congruity with other miracles, and its obvious improbability. It is incongruous, because a standing miracle of this sort, wrought, apart from any religious end, in a great city like Jerusalem, is altogether *unlike* anything else recorded. It is improbable, because Josephus, who would only have been too proud to boast of this mark of the Divine favour to the Jews, makes no mention of it. The view taken of the matter by many commentators is, that the angel referred to was a messenger from the temple who at stated seasons stirred up the blood received there from the sacrifices, and that this was popularly supposed to possess healing virtues.

The opinions of wise and good men, again, regarding demoniacs are various, and so long as they do not limit the power of God or explain away that which is written they are innocent. The darkness at the Crucifixion, objected to by Gibbon as asserting an eclipse which did not then take place, Guizot, following Origen, shows to be in all probability a preternatural darkness occasioned in the atmosphere. But all these varieties of opinion entertained by men who in common hold to the essential verity of Scripture as a Divine revelation, only go to show how frank and fearless has been the criticism to which the Book has been subjected, and how willing many Christians are *in the strength of their faith* to deal with it without any unfair reserve.

5. The objection that doctrines are taught in the Bible which are inconsistent either with the justice or

the love of God cannot be sustained. That such are frequently *inferred from* the sacred text is true enough; but these conclusions belong to the interpretation of the Book by man, not to what it reveals as from God. It has certainly yet to be proved that any doctrine of election bearing on the world to come, is to be found in the Bible, that is different in principle from that which, as a fact of life, obtains in the providential government of God on earth, viz. the selection of some even before birth to rank and wealth, while others are introduced only to poverty and degradation. *The end*—however much it may be evaded or lost sight of on earth—being, in both worlds, that by this means all may be benefited, some by giving and some by receiving. The *few* are favoured, only that by their loving self-sacrifice the *many* may be more favoured. That it is often not so now, is no evidence that it will not be so in 'the new earth wherein dwelleth *righteousness*.'

The dogma of the Eternal sensitive suffering of those who are unconverted *here*, which has descended to us from the apostasy has, we firmly believe, no place in the Word of God; it is, at the best, but a human and very inaccurate theological inference.

Even on the doctrine of the Trinity—for the word itself is not Scriptural—much has been said and written which can find no sanction in the Bible. Scripture indeed bids us see in THE FATHER, the Eternal Will creating and governing all things, Omnipotent, Omniscient, and Omnipresent; in THE WORD, God communicating with man, declaring the Divine Will to him and becoming incarnate for his redemption; and in THE HOLY SPIRIT eternal life and love working out the

Divine designs whether in creation or redemption; but it tells us also that these are ONE. There it leaves us; for the nature or mode of an eternal triplicity in the Divine nature is far beyond the comprehension of finite minds. Nor is it too much to say that the progress of truth has been greatly hindered by metaphysical distinctions, often utterly unmeaning, regarding the Divine existence; as well as by expressions which, although embodying more or less that which is true, are in themselves unauthorised.

To apply to Christ such terms as 'Very God of very God, begotten not made;' to speak of 'God the Son and God the Holy Ghost;' of 'three persons but one God,' and such like, however needful in scholastic controversy, or whatever amount of truth they may embody, cannot be justified by apostolic habits of thought and expression. These phrases too often occasion the very evil they are intended to meet, and very frequently distress and perplex tender souls by creating difficulties which would otherwise never be felt. But 'fools rush in where angels fear to tread.'

Dr. Irons seems to imagine that the absence from Scripture of such words as 'Trinity,' 'Holy Orders,' 'Holy Sacrament,' 'Priest,' and such like, is fatal to those who regard the Bible as their only guide. 'What,' he says, 'is to become of all these to the man whose criticised Bible is his revelation?'[1] Whether or no eternal punishment is taught *in Scripture* he admits has been made 'fairly debateable.'[2] But one thought meets all difficulty. 'Him whom we ignorantly worship, the Church declares unto us by her creeds, her sacraments,

[1] The Bible and its Interpreters, p. 67. [2] Ibid. pp. 94, 96.

and her hierarchy, and these things,' he holds, 'come into being quite apart from St. Matthew's Gospel, or St. Paul's Epistle to the Romans, or the Revelation of St. John.' So broad is the distinction between the Bible and Church authority; so needful is it to keep in mind that in defending the one we have nothing to do with any perplexities arising out of the other.

6. The last difficulty to be looked at is the supposed *unintelligibility* of Scripture, shown by the division of opinion to which it has given rise among those who study it diligently and earnestly. This is, by far, the most serious difficulty of all, and would indeed be fatal to the pretensions of the book as containing a message from God to man, if it could also be shown that *the cause* of the divisions in question is to be found in the darkness of the document rather than in the prejudices and worldly interests of its expositors. But this cannot be done. No such diversity existed originally, and it exists now only as a result of that great and disastrous falling away which Paul foresaw and predicted (2 Thess. ii. 7).

To imagine, as so many do, that Romanism, or Lutheranism, or Anglicanism, or any other particular form of organised Christianity, embodies in itself this evil thing is absurd. The 'Mystery of Iniquity,' it is clear enough, *worked* in apostolic days, as it has worked ever since, viz. through the corruption of religion by its association with secular advantages. Whether these come in the shape of money, or of power, of popularity, or of status matters little. 'I know,' says Paul to the elders of the Ephesians, 'that after my departing shall grievous wolves enter in among you, not sparing the flock' (Acts xx. 29). Already, he says, there are many 'who *make a traffic of the word*,' for so Archbishop Trench translates the second of Corinthians (ii. 17). 'Beware,' he writes to the Colossians, 'lest any man *make booty of you*, through philosophy'—scientific and systematic theology so called (Col. ii. 8). 'Woe unto them,' exclaims Jude, for 'they have run greedily after the error of Balaam *for reward*' (v. 11). 'Withdraw thyself,' says Paul to Timothy, from men of corrupt minds who suppose that 'gain is godliness;' or rather, according to Dr. Trench, that 'godliness is lucre—a means of getting gain' (1 Tim. vi. 5).

Very startling indeed is it to find that at so early a period, and at a time when one would have thought that persecution and death were the only rewards that awaited the minister of Christ, the germ at least of coming greed and ambition should have been traceable. Yet so it was; teaching us at least this lesson, that no outward circumstances, however apparently favourable to purity, can altogether hinder designing men from usurping authority over conscience, or getting gain out of persons who are capable of being bribed by the promise of ease.

But how, it will perhaps be said, does this fact, if it be one, account for the all but endless diversity of opinion which exists as to what the Bible really teaches?—for this is the point with which we have now to deal.

The reply is obvious. Ecclesiastical bodies, whatever may be their character—whether ruling a state or ruled by it, whether established or voluntary, whether bond or free—cannot exist without, in one form or other, requiring adherence to church authority in matters of faith. Some—as Episcopalians or Presbyterians—enforce by subscription that particular form of thought which is embodied in their articles or catechism. Some, like the Wesleyans, require a more general but not less stringent adherence to the writings of their great founder. Others, as Independents or Baptists, cast anchor on Puritan ground. ALL, without exception, fix beforehand the great outline of belief, expressed or understood, which must be accepted before any man can share the privileges, or derive benefit from the emoluments which belong to the church or congregation in which he may desire to minister. *As a rule*, the preacher is specially educated in and required to abide by the dogmas of the particular sect for whose service he is intended. Differences are in this way perpetuated.

And here let us, once for all, decidedly protest against the line of argument we are pursuing being construed into an attack either on the creeds or the government of the Church of England, or regarded as an assault on any Church or body of ministers either in our own country or elsewhere. This is not the place to carry on such a warfare, were it either needful or desirable to do so. But it is not. We are answering the objections of the sceptic not to the Church but to the Bible; and if, in doing so, we are compelled to separate the one from the other, and in the interests of truth obliged to put aside everything in the world, beyond the Book we have undertaken to defend, this, instead of being matter of complaint, should be cheerfully acquiesced in by those who profess to regard every other interest as unimportant when brought into comparison with that of the Word of God.

The Church and the Bible have not always needed separate defenders. It is granted by all parties—'by the thoroughly evangelical Count de Gasparin, by the liberal Neander, and by the Roman Catholic Möhler'—that among the earliest disciples 'there was not the remotest desire to unravel the puzzles which afterwards beset the theological world. There is in their child-like faith an utter unconsciousness of them. With regard to outward forms the apostles verged towards indifference. They did not look on baptism as of great consequence; and they regarded the observance of the eucharist as binding on them, because it was a memorial instituted by Him who was their life, and the object of intensest love. In the administration of their communities there ruled one great principle, viz., that each Christian man was a king and a priest—that by the indwelling of Christ's spirit within him he had become a free man in the highest sense of the word. The organization of churches under different office-bearers might proceed in various ways, provided this principle were untouched—and in fact the offices in the church, if they might be called offices, were not fixed, established modes of government, but wise methods of bringing every gift of the church into active employment.'[1] If, therefore, it should *seem* to any that we have reflected on modern Churches, let it be borne in mind that we have done so unwillingly, and only to remove occasions of stumbling out of the way.

Our only anxiety is that in considering difficulties in Scripture, men should not attribute to the Book that

[1] Donaldson's History of Christian Literature and Doctrine, vol. i. pp. 50–52.

which really does not belong to it. Forgetfulness of this distinction has led a recent writer to maintain—surely without any good reason—that 'the doctrines which the great mass of Christians *have drawn from the* Bible, for eighteen centuries, must either be what God meant them to draw, or else He did not inspire the Book. One thing or other, it is said, must hold—the old sense of the old words, or else the admission that they were not miraculously given by the Creator of the human mind for its instruction.' All this of course proceeds on the supposition—favoured alike by believers and by sceptics—that one of the greatest historical facts in the world may be altogether ignored, viz., the existence and influence of a departure from the faith, which, working unseen during the later portions of the apostolic age, rapidly developed after the decease of the last member of the sacred college into that 'mystery of iniquity' which culminated in Rome, and which has ever since dominated over by far the largest portion of Christendom, flinging its shadow to this day, more or less, upon all of us. To the surprising transformation wrought in all lands by this undergrowth of error in the garden of the Lord, Dean Stanley has beautifully alluded in his introductory lecture on 'Ecclesiastical History.'

It is, we are aware, commonly urged in extenuation of our religious diversities that the differences of Christians as to doctrine are not so great as they seem; that the confessions of the reformed of different countries are, after all, very similar; that even Romanism maintains a body of truth which is common to all true believers; and there are those, we doubt not, who will blame us for not having brought this fact forward as a sufficient answer to the objection of the sceptic. We cannot do so, because it does not satisfy our own mind. The various Churches of Christendom are, as a fact, united in opinion only so far as they have followed in common the theological systems of Augustine or of Anselm. The agreement, therefore, in question, so far as it goes, is hereditary and traditional only, and not the result of that humble but independent investigation which is alone of value. That *a common Christian life* underlies all sorts of opinions is true enough, but this is not the point under consideration.

CHAPTER IX.

INTERPRETATION OF SCRIPTURE.

Whether it be *possible* to separate the defence of the Bible as a document from all considerations relative to the mode in which the Book should be interpreted, may be regarded as an open question. It is, however, not easy to see how such a separation can be absolute, so long as the view we take of *the contents* of Scripture more or less biases our decision as to the Divine character of the record, or so long as our method of interpreting that record depends, to some extent at least, on the opinion we form regarding its inspiration.

If the whole Book be inspired in that plenary sense which excludes the possibility of error, interpretation, as Dr. Chalmers somewhere says, clearly resolves itself into mere questions of grammar. On the contrary, if the supernatural character of the revelation be denied, and the Book comes to be regarded simply as the expression of the combined genius and piety of the writers, *then* its meaning will naturally be sought rather in the light of its supposed correspondence with the highest intuitions of the reader, than in any study of its grammatical construction. Further, if it is viewed only or chiefly as a revelation of general principles, which are to be logically developed and arranged by divines according to the order of their importance, *then* systematic theology, or the interpretation of the Church springs into existence, and with it, in one form or other, the assumption of authority.

The sense of uncertainty which, in the present day, has come over so many devout and believing minds as to *the teaching* of the Bible, is to be attributed partly, no doubt, to the different conclusions of systematic theologians, each system claiming to be sustained by Scripture, and, therefore, to be positively true; partly to fanciful expositions founded on the notion that Scripture is given us *to be developed*, and that hidden meanings are in this way to be brought out of it; and partly to a particular kind of textual preaching, originating, no doubt, in a somewhat superstitious view of verbal inspiration, which demands that we should dwell on every word of the text, as if the very syllables possessed something like a magic power of their own. Any book thus treated must necessarily soon be disencumbered of all definite meaning, and its teaching be placed at the mercy of its expositors. Such has in fact been the experience of the past.[1]

But while Divine revelation can have but one true meaning, nothing can be more certain than that, being a message from the Heavenly Father to His erring and sinful creatures, it must have a power of adaptation to each and all of them in particular, which, from the very nature of the case, forbids any exhaustive or authoritative interpretation of its contents. It has been truly said of Shakspeare that he was a 'myriad-minded' man.

[1] See Appendix, Note B. 'Biblical Interpretation.'

How much more may it be said of the Bible, that it is a myriad-minded book. Perhaps it is not too much to affirm that, being intended to find affinity with every possible variety of thought and feeling; to adapt itself to every man's separate idiosyncrasy; to reveal to each just that particular phase or form of truth which is needful for him or her; which can alone be made practical and powerful for good to him or her; it is as impossible that it should have any one given and stereotyped expression, as that it should teach to every man one given and stereotyped lesson.

Yet, let it never be forgotten that this peculiarity by no means interferes with the *definiteness* of the message, or in any way tends either to impair its explicitness, or to necessitate an authorized interpretation. For only as Scripture is allowed to adapt itself to the peculiar mental and moral condition of each individual, do its words become 'spirit and life' to him, ruling his conduct and reigning in his affections. Instead, therefore, of finding an occasion of stumbling in the fact that diversities of view on many points, always have, and probably always will characterise Christians, we might rather discover in the wonderful adaptation of Divine teaching to each, evidence of the source from which it comes. For it is at once one, and yet diverse; unchanging, and yet endowed with a capacity of all but infinite fitness to every variety of character.

Just as material light, although the same to all, is yet different to persons of imperfect vision, suffering under diverse forms of disease; so is spiritual illumination a different thing to men in different stages of the divine life, with varying intellectual powers, and, above all, with conflicting wills, passions, and interests; and just as it would be impossible so to temper the light of the sun, that it should leave precisely the same impression on every optic nerve, whether sound or otherwise, so is it neither possible nor desirable that Divine truth should come home to the man who is jaundiced by his prejudices, or drugged by his sins, precisely as it does to the simple and righteous soul who desires *to know*, only that he may love and obey.

Nevertheless, to repeat what we have just said, we should greatly err if we argued from this peculiarity of revelation that it had no one definite and true meaning; that it had more than one; or that it ever was intended to be handled as a nucleus, around which ingenious illustration, varied reasoning, and imaginative eloquence might gather, for the delectation of a mixed crowd of auditors. Nor do we less mistake when we seize upon this or any other feature of Holy Scripture, either for the purpose of excusing our divisions, or as a reason for endeavoring after a false and deceptive unity, by requiring the acceptance of any given proposition, or series of propositions, deduced by the skill of man *from* the statements of the Book. There is no real unity on earth, whether in the natural or in the spiritual economy, which does not *consist in* diversity.

'Inspired teaching,' says Dr. Archer Butler, 'explain it as we may, appears comparatively indifferent to what seems to us so peculiarly important—close logical connection, and the intellectual symmetry of doctrines.' How much, he adds, 'is sometimes conveyed by assumptions, such as inspiration alone can make without any violation of the canons of reasoning!—*for with it alone assertion is argument.*' Had this truth been borne in mind we should have escaped many a discussion on fate and free will, and been content to know that while, as creatures, we are necessarily dependent on God for everything, we have yet free will enough to be capable, under Divine teaching, of *voluntarily* choosing the good and rejecting the evil; that life and death, sin and grace, time and eternity, all bear on the grand result of this voluntary choice; that as its accomplishment on earth, in spite of all hindrances, in the hearts of *some* is the present reward of the Redeemer's sufferings, its accomplishment hereafter on *the many* will be the final triumph of Divine wisdom and love.

Traditional interpretation denies this. It allows, indeed, that, 'as by the disobedience of one man *the many* were made sinners, so, by the obedience of One shall *the many* be made righteous;' that the world, though a fallen, is a redeemed world; that Christ will eventually destroy the works of the devil; that good is destined, in the long run, to overcome evil; and that one day 'every knee shall bow' to Him who is 'King of kings, and Lord of lords.' But it does so only under many limitations. It is slow, if not unwilling, to admit even the restoration of those who have here lived and died without even hearing of a Saviour. It looks for a counterpoise to the losses of the past in the salvation of infants, and in the possible prolongation of a millennial period until the number of the saved shall exceed the number of the lost; an arithmetical way of treating human happiness and misery which has in all ages found plenty of admirers, although anything less Godlike can scarcely be conceived. Divine revelation, however, is not responsible for this perversity.

The Gospel, as Christ presents it, is, in one form or other, good news not to the few only but to all men without exception; to the heathen as well as to the Christian; to the Jew in his impenitence; to the profligate in his sin; to the ignorant in his darkness; and to the sceptic in his unbelief. Not a word intimates that its entire value hangs either on the knowledge or on the belief of it by those for whose benefit it was announced. It is a declaration of what God *will do*; not of what He is willing to do if man permit. If it were not so, human nature being what it is, and the world what it always has been, the message *would be, to by far the greater portion of mankind*, of no avail whatever; the consolations it offers would be, to most persons, absolutely unreal, and the mission of Christ, instead of being a redeeming one, would involve little more than the ratification of a curse.

Yet the Gospel is not *alike* to all; for it has a *special* object to accomplish as well as a general one. 'God, who is the Saviour of all men, is, we are distinctly told, *specially* the Saviour of them that believe' (1 Tim. iv. 10).

The *mode* in which this double result will be accomplished is not fully explained to us, but the declaration is not the less true on that account. Some things in Divine revelation are written as with a sunbeam; other things are only *hinted at*. Yet who shall dare to say that the one is not as certain as the other? As it is in Nature, so is it in Scripture: some things are proclaimed as from the mountain top; other things are only whispered to the listening ear. The one *arrests* attention; the other *rewards* it. Some things are needful to be known for present guidance; other things are opened up as a recompense to those who desire to gain a full understanding of all the ways of God, so far as He may please to let us become acquainted with them. Yet all alike demand the scrutiny of the wise, and all alike reward the diligence of the industrious.

That the Bible has a twofold purpose to accomplish in the world is evident from its character. If in one aspect it addresses itself to *man as man* everywhere, in another it speaks *only to a particular class* of men, viz., to those who, knowing the voice of the Redeemer, have received Him into their hearts, and believed on Him to the saving of their souls. To the one it announces, 'Glad tidings of great joy, which shall be to all (the) people.' Its note is, 'On earth peace, good will toward men.'[1] To the other it says, 'Think not that I am come to send peace on earth. I came not to send peace but a sword.'[2]

To *the many* it speaks not only of that silent abode where the slave shall be free from his master, where the wicked cease from troubling, and where the weary are at rest; it points also to a world where 'there shall be neither sorrow nor any more pain.'[3] To *the few* it says, 'All things are yours,' whether 'life or death,' whether 'things present or things to come,' all are yours, for ye are Christ's, and Christ is God's.[4] To *both* it reveals a day when reconciliation between God and man being

[1] Luke ii. 10–14.
[2] Matt. x. 34.
[3] Rev. xxi. 4.
[4] 1 Cor. iii. 21 and 22.

perfected there shall be 'new heavens and a new earth, wherein dwelleth righteousness.'[1]

To all it proclaims a Father, little recognised, but not the less loving, who asks of every man the obedience and affection which is so sinfully withheld; but *to some* it speaks of an 'earnest of the Spirit' already possessed, and of a present heaven, enjoyed even on earth, although accompanied by many sorrows, and oftentimes by great tribulation.

These, always said to be 'a little flock,' and 'a peculiar people,' are spoken of as having received 'power or privilege to become the sons of God' *in a special sense*; they are 'born from above,' born 'not of blood nor of the will of the flesh, but of God.'[2] Penitent and pardoned, they are declared to be even now 'heirs of God, and joint heirs with Christ;' they are styled 'elect and chosen;' they are said to be 'predestinated from the foundation of the world, that they might be holy and without blame before God in love;' they are to 'reign in life;' they are to be 'kings and priests to God and to Christ for ever and ever.' Nor should it be forgotten that it is *to these* that the fearful warnings which are by preachers generally applied to the ungodly are in the text really addressed. In all these cases *the message is emphatically to a class.*

Broader distinctions than those referred to it is scarcely possible to lay down. Confusions more disastrous than those which arise when these distinctions are disregarded can scarcely be imagined. Yet these confusions pervade Christian society, and are propagated with untiring zeal both from the pulpit and the press.

[1] 2 Pet. iii. 13. [2] John i. 12, 13.

The consequence is, that while some regard the offers of the Gospel as addressed only to the elect, and others look upon the glad tidings as finding adequate fulfilment in the general improvement of society, in advancing civilisation, and in material progress, most persons, blending the two, reduce the high demands made upon the Christian, as *a man not of this world*, to the level of humanity in general, and regard them as imperative only so far as they are workable in ordinary Christianised society.

The line drawn, however, *in Scripture*, is a very sharp one and easily defined. On the one side of it stand not only nominal believers, but the vast multitudes who, in all past ages as now, have either never heard of Christ, or heard of Him only in connection with superstitions that have misled, assumptions that have disgusted, or sectarianisms that have repelled. On the other side of the line are to be found *all*, by whatever name they may be known, who, having listened to the call to immediate repentance and faith, have been led by the grace of God earnestly to regard and honestly to obey it.

To *both* these classes a day of judgment is announced; a day when each shall receive according to what he has done in the body, whether it be good or bad, and therefore *to all* essentially a judgment of works. But not in the same sense. Of the *one* we are told that they shall not come into condemnation with the world. To the faithful among them, though it be but in 'few' things, is to be committed 'many things.' Reward *bestowed* will be the recompense of their faith and steadfastness. Reward *withheld* will be the punishment of their negligence and sin. Of the *other* it is said that they shall be judged every man according to his opportunities and actual doings, some being beaten with 'few stripes,' and some with 'many stripes.'

Of the finally reprobate we will not here speak. It *may* be that there are men so depraved that they *cannot* be saved from themselves and from their sins, without the application of forces which are inconsistent with the retention of that amount of moral freedom, apart from which what we call *character* cannot exist—a *possibility* which duly pondered may perhaps throw light on the 'lake of fire' and 'the second death.'

Such, as it appears to us, is the teaching of Scripture, when regarded without reference to the dogmas of Churches or of sects; and if, as we stated at the beginning of this chapter, the view we take of *the contents* of the Bible more or less biases our decision as to the Divine character of the record, it is not too much to ask that the aspect of it now presented may be *weighed* before it is rejected.

Corresponding to the *twofold message* we have indicated is the *twofold form* in which, as a fact, the Gospel is constantly bearing upon mankind: viz., as *an influence in society*, alleviating human sorrow, modifying institutions, quickening benevolence, and generally elevating public sentiment, and as a *power from above*, transforming the individual believer, delivering him from the dominion of evil, and making him to feel that, like his Lord, he is but a pilgrim and a stranger here.

Recognised or unrecognised, these two forms of action are constantly going on, sometimes separately embodied with more or less distinctness in regularly organised institutions, and sometimes blending in Churches of various forms and character. *The one*, which has been called that of multitudinism, would seem naturally to belong to national establishments of religion; *the other*, that of individualism, as naturally to nonconformity. Nor can it be doubted that if each of these classes (*as religious men*—for we have here nothing to do with any man's duty as a citizen) was to pursue its own calling of God, regardless of everything else—if each could carry out the distinctive principle it embodies without rivalry, the measure of truth thus separately conserved would be brought to bear upon the world with far more force than it can be amid the strifes and ambitions which now so frequently characterise both parties. If each has indeed a religious idea to embody, each will of course find its strength in the extent to which it realizes that particular end to which its principles point. Rivalry, leading to imitation, as it now so often does, can never be of any real service to either, and still less to the world at large.[1]

Rightly ordered, the one might teach us our obligations as a Christian people; the other, our privileges as the children of God. The former, fulfilling the mission of the Baptist, would call every man to repentance. The latter, recognizing growth, would teach the sacredness of religious convictions, and hold up *individuality* as the law of the spiritual life. The first, whether working through creeds and confessions, by the press or by the pulpit, by authority or by oratorical appeal, would seek to awaken, to rouse, and to guide. The last, recognising the fact that he who has become Christ's has, by

[1] See Appendix, Note C. 'National Establishments.'

that affiance, been forever taken out of the hand of man, would seek to cherish the spiritual independence of the renewed soul, and teach that to no higher elevation can any man reach than to that which he rises when he becomes THE SCHOLAR OF GOD.

There may, however, still be those who fail to see that any particular interpretation of Scripture, whatever may be its merits or demerits, can have very much to do with the acceptance or rejection of the Book supposed to be thus read or misread. The question, therefore, must be dealt with as one of fact. Such persons must be content to believe on testimony, whatever their own experience may be, that in many cases interpretation has a great deal to do with the acceptance or rejection of the document. The letter which has been prefixed to this volume may be regarded as a witness. For *there*, as among men generally, the Bible is clearly held responsible for dogmas which it does not teach, the Gospel being not unfrequently rejected because, among other things, it is supposed to consign all but a mere fraction of the human race to eternal wickedness and misery.

That such is *not* the fact can of course only be proved by an appeal from man to God—from the commentary to the text—from the traditions of the Church to the true sayings of the Holy Ghost; but this, of course, involves interpretation. Other evidence might be adduced, if it were needful, to show that the connection between prevailing unbelief and ordinary orthodox theology is not an imaginary one. The late Mr. Isaac Taylor, than whom no one has a better right to speak on this subject, has distinctly avowed his conviction that *the only effectual remedy* for modern scepticism is to be found 'in

AN INTELLIGIBLE AND DEFENSIBLE PRINCIPLE OF BIBLICAL INTERPRETATION.'

'Until this is obtained,' he says, 'Christianity will be found powerless against infidelity.' Those who have watched the current of public opinion carefully and closely, know well—much as they may dislike the conclusion or shrink from the avowal of it—that 'the growing feeling that prevails, amid all the splendours of advancing science, that this is but the night-time of the soul,' can only be relieved by 'a thorough and absolute deliverance of the Bible from the trammels that have been imposed upon it by polemical theology.'[1]

[1] The Restoration of Belief.

CHAPTER X.

THE MODERN PHARISEE.

By the 'Pharisee' is here meant the man who—like his prototype of old—first attaches a superstitious importance to the letter of Scripture, and then adds to it a crowd of theological inferences, sometimes based on the authority of 'fathers,' and sometimes developed on principles of interpretation which permit the expositor to tread in the footsteps of those Jewish rabbis who made mountains of meaning to hang on the plainest statements.

Pharisees—whatever may be their personal excellence—are, in relation to the Bible, mainly ruled by old prejudices; they delight in whatever is *fixed*, whether by authority or by the common opinion of Christians. They insist that reverence for the past is *commanded* in Scripture, since we are told to 'ask for the old paths;' that submission to the opinions of the good is *enforced*, since we are bidden to follow 'the footsteps of the flock.' The connection in which these passages may stand is with such persons a matter of very little moment. To question their applicability is but to indicate the unhallowed consequences which flow from the exercise of private judgment. To such men the plenary inspiration of the Bible is the *first article*, if not the foundation of their faith. With most of them the authority of the Church to expound the volume is the complement of their belief.

That this idea, however expressed or embodied, carries with it not only the denial to revelation of its self-evidencing nature, as light coming from God to man, but also a casting away of the birthright of the Christian as a child of the light, never seems to enter the minds of these good men. They wonder that so many, whom they cannot but regard as true followers of the Redeemer, should revolt against this 'disinheriting' process. They cannot see that blind submission to authority, instead of being identical with faith and humility, is a very different thing from either the one or the other. They forget that the filial spirit is to trust *the Father*, not the stranger or even the brother. They forget that to be childlike is not to be childish, and that Rome has taught us there is no limit to the surrender that will be demanded if once we yield to any man the right of *discerning for us* what is true and what is false.

Let us, however, inquire what can be said for the theory—since it is nothing more—that the Bible from Genesis to Revelation is inspired and infallible.

The latest, and in some respects the most elaborate, defence of the infallibility of the Bible *as a book* will probably be found in a volume of sermons by Mr. Burgon, preached before the University of Oxford soon after the publication of 'Essays and Reviews.' In reading that work, as well as various other publications taking similar ground, one is certainly startled to find not how much, but how very little, can be advanced in favour either of the verbal or plenary inspiration of Scripture. Everything important in the enquiry seems to be *assumed.*

The ground taken is, 'The verbal inspiration of the Bible is an axiom, a first truth from which all others start.' The conclusions of those who advocate this theory do not, of course, embrace either the denial of various readings or the imperfections of translations, but it is difficult to see how the admission of the one or the performance of the other can be consistent with the theory so much valued.

The form in which these views are commonly put is something like this: Our Lord has said, 'the Scripture cannot be broken' (explained away—so Alford on John x. 35), *therefore everything* in the volume called by us the Bible is inspired and 'infallible.' Or thus: 'prophets and apostles claim, and justly, to deliver God-breathed messages; *therefore* historians, whether narrators of what they had seen or copyists from public records, must necessarily possess the same Divine gift.' Or again: Jesus prayed for His apostles, saying, 'sanctify them by Thy truth, Thy word is truth;' *therefore* everything regarded as Scripture in our Lord's time is God's revealed truth. That the Septuagint then contained portions of the Apocrypha they do not think it worth while to notice. *That* is one course of reasoning.

A second is this: 'If the *authorship* of each book is not accurately stated, the truthfulness of its contents departs.' Mr. Burgon says, 'If the son of Nun did not write the book which goes under his name, *then* the narrative is not authentic.' If any distinction be drawn between the inspired and the uninspired in Scripture, then everything belonging to the latter category must be cast out. That which is stated may be perfectly true; the man who records it may have been an ear or an eye witness of what he tells us; nevertheless, if he has not been inspired in such a sense as to render any inaccuracy impossible, his words are worthless. 'We refuse,' Mr. Burgon goes on to say, 'to retain a single passage which is not (in the highest sense) the Word of God.' Not only must the message itself be inspired and infallible, every accessory to it must, in the same way, be inspired also. Refusing to allow that a given thought may be both truthfully and accurately expressed in varying words, he says, 'as for thoughts being inspired without the words, you may as well talk of a tune without notes or a sum without figures.'

These extravagancies, for such we cannot but think them, are supposed to find support in reasonings like these. 'Admit the slightest difference as to the infallibility of different portions of the Bible and you make every man a judge as to what he will receive and what he will reject.' Such a man must 'take a pen and cross out every word he imagines to be uninspired, in which case how can we know that he does not cross out texts on which we rest our hopes?' Such is the second line of argument.

But there is a third which amounts to this: 'Christ and His apostles quoted from the Old Testament, *therefore* every part of the Book from which they quoted is certainly inspired.' Further, where Christ and His apostles *apply* Scripture, the text thus used must originally have had hidden within it the particular truth it is used to illustrate; e. g. 'If Deuteronomy xxv. 4 has no reference to the Christian ministry, *then* the entire context in two of St. Paul's Epistles (1 Corinthians ix. 9; 1 Timothy v. 18) must go at once.' Further still: if Paul shows, as he does, that certain Scriptures may be applied allegorically, *all Scripture* must have a depth of meaning far beyond that which appears; in consequence, all of it is inspired, and it is our duty to bring out hidden meanings from everything, whatever may be the end for which it was primarily given. 'Even mere catalogues of names,' insists Mr. Burgon, 'are full of edification, the driest details full of God. The list of the dukes of Edom is as much inspired, and in the same sense, as every other part.'[1] This is the third line of reasoning.

It is always difficult to state the views of an opponent in what he would consider a fair and full manner, and it is quite possible that this has not been accomplished in the present instance. But if it be so, the defect is unintentional.

Easy is it to understand how all this inconclusive discourse *about* inspiration may be to many pious persons wonderfully attractive. They will say it is such *a simple* view, so straightforward and reverential, so humbling to man's reason, so needful for his guidance, that to reject it is as dishonouring to God as it is indicative of human pride. Whether it be a true view or not seems scarcely worthy of consideration. To doubt on such a matter is to sin.

The answer to such declamation is, however, obvious. The view in question is a *mere theory*, and certainly not the less so because the persons who hold it are continually telling us *they* have no theory of inspiration—they *believe* in it, and that is enough. The question is, *why*

[1] Gaussen says of the entire Bible: 'In its miraculous pages *every verse and word*, without exception, even to a particle apparently the most indifferent, must have been given of God.'

do they believe in what is called the verbal inspiration of Scripture? That the Word of God is *embodied in the Bible* is here, at least, not disputed; that, as they put it, 'to impute blunders to the Holy Ghost is an impiety,' cannot, surely, be denied; that 'to bow before a Divine statement without question becomes us as creatures far better than stumbling at it,' every Christian must allow; but does it thence follow that *everything* found within the volume which contains God's word is as sacred and as infallible as that word itself? This is the real point in question.

Many think otherwise; they cannot bring themselves to believe that it is either safe or reverent *to assume* without adequate evidence that anything is properly speaking Divine which is contrary to what is elsewhere revealed of God, anything which, when examined and tested by the light Christ has given us, is incapable of defence. Well may such persons ask, 'Is it right to stake the truthfulness of the Bible on the accuracy or otherwise of the account we have of its authorship, or, indeed, on any literary question whatever? Is it either wise or just to affirm that the *exact substance* of a statement, the *real purport* of what may have been spoken, is not for all practical purposes the same thing as the very words which were actually uttered?' Too much is at issue to render these enquiries other than of vital importance.

The question of *hidden meanings* is a more delicate one to deal with, for if we must of necessity hold that every text (those quoted by the Evangelist Matthew, for instance) had in it *originally* the signification which is there by accommodation implied; if the writer brings each several passage from the Old Testament before us, *not* as an illustration, refulfilment, or reapplication of what had occurred long before, *not* as an accommodation in any sense, but simply as a development; if we are to believe that the beautiful image of Rachel weeping for her children was intended by him who first used it as a mystic prophecy of the massacre at Bethlehem; if the words of Hosea, 'Out of Egypt have I called my son,' embody a distinct prophecy of the flight of Joseph: *then* it may readily be granted the Bible assumes a character which obliges us to admit our utter incapacity to understand even its plainest narratives.

Further, if we are bound to interpret the Old Testament *generally*, as St. Paul *in some cases* interprets it; if we are to find in every historical personage a type of Christ; if we are to say of each great event that is recorded, 'which thing is an allegory,' and to expound accordingly: *then*, undoubtedly, we must regard every part of the Bible without exception as inspired, infallible, and alas! it must be added, unintelligible. Nothing can be plainer than that, if this be the case, no uninspired man is capable of interpreting the Bible; for who would consent to be, in this respect, at the mercy of one who, for aught we can tell, may be fanciful, ingenious, or weak? Under such methods Mr. Jowett is right in saying, 'we may shut our lexicons and draw lots for the sense.' The Jewish rabbis, by following such a course without the qualification required—infallible guidance—made, as our Lord Himself tells us, 'the word of God of none effect.' One of them, it is said, actually professed to teach thirteen different methods of expounding the plainest declarations. Short of inspiration, it is obviously impossible that any man should be qualified to interpret Scripture *if he is to develop* what he assumes to be truth out of the Book, instead of being content to accept what he *finds* there.

The only answer to all this is THE CHURCH. God, we are told, has provided for all difficulty by giving to His Church—whether represented by popes or councils, by fathers or by common consent, matters not—*power and authority* to settle all disputed points, and to declare to the people the true meaning of the written Word.

Mr. Burgon soon finds himself obliged to fall back upon this doctrine. 'God,' he says, 'vouchsafes to His Church effectual guidance. Want of faith in the Church (by which he understands the Church of England) and her ordinances is the first step in a soul's downward progress.' To imagine oneself a disciple of Christ or Paul, and so to disengage oneself from the history of Christendom and the after-thoughts of theology is, he thinks, 'inordinate conceit.' The creeds, he assures us, are older than Scripture. The doctrines of the Church were not *found* in Scripture; they existed before it, and are only proved by it. He speaks of these creeds as 'coeval with Christianity itself,' and as bearing 'a solemn independent testimony from the very birthday of Christianity.' He thinks it monstrous to suppose that a man is either at liberty or able to gather his own religion for himself out of the Bible. Nor are we, in England, he says, thus left. 'The book of Common Prayer is a sufficient safeguard.'

Nor is he alone in this view. Another distinguished man, although certainly of a very different school—Dr. Rowland Williams—tells us that the Church is 'an inspired society;' that 'the Prayer Book is constructed on this idea;' and that the Bible, like the liturgy, is 'the written voice of the congregation.' So strangely do extremes sometimes meet.

It may not be unadvisable here to separate the germ of truth which is found in these observations from the mass of error by which it is surrounded. No one disputes that the Church (that is, a company of living believers in Christ) was called into existence by the Lord and His Apostles *before* the New Testament was written; but it owes this existence to the word which the Scriptures *contain*. 'The word was antecedent to the existence of the Church, as the cause is to the effect. The *writing* of that Word, and its reception when written, were subsequent to the formation of the Church (the Christian congregation of believers), but the writing only *made permanent* for future time the Word by which the Church had been created; and the reception of the writings only *recognised* them as the same Word in its form of permanence. Thus, while the Church is *chronologically before* the Bible, the Bible is *potentially* before the Church; since the *written* Word, which is the ground of faith to later generations, is one in origin, authority, and substance with the *oral* Word, which was the ground of faith to the first generation of Christians.'[1]

Of course, neither these facts nor any reasoning founded thereon, will have weight with persons, and they are many, who are determined, at all hazards, to uphold ecclesiastical authority; still less with those who tell us that the theological theories and peculiar views of Paul and John—although worthy of respect

[1] Bernard's Bampton Lectures.

because worked out with much painful thought—are in no respects *revelation*, or at all binding upon others. For here again extremes meet. The *Sceptic*, classing *apostolic* developments with those of a later age, necessarily plays into the hands of those who maintain a continual inspiration in the Church, and in so doing, whatever he may intend, practically supports its claim to an authority which, if not absolute, is paramount to every other. Some *Churchmen* on the other hand, it may be feared, by the arrogance they often manifest, as well as by the unreasonableness of the pretensions they put forth, drive thoughtful men into scepticism—a result for which such persons care little, so long as the esoteric unbelief is concealed by an exoteric respect for ecclesiastics.

And here it is that Romanism harmonises with some extreme forms of Anglicanism, to an extent that may well prepare the way for reunion. Articles, as we have seen, can be easily explained away; Ritualistic observances may be practised in common; misunderstandings may, without difficulty, be removed; *all* obstacles, in short, may soon be got out of the way, if only it is admitted that there is a perpetual inspiration in the Church, carrying with it, of course, everything that is necessarily connected therewith. For if, as this theory supposes, theology is a science, and like other sciences, progressive; yet progress, as Dr. Dollinger puts it, 'not like that of chemistry—since there can be no discovery of new facts, from which we are to induce new laws; but a progress analogous to that of geometry —since it consists in the gradual evolution of the fundamental ideas, the discovery of new relations involved in them, and new spheres in which they are valid;' if, we repeat, this be granted, everything is yielded; since only authorised teachers, enjoying the perpetual inspiration assumed to be in the Church, can be fit to evolve fundamental ideas, to discover new relations, or to decide on the new spheres in which they are valid. On this showing, the subjection of mankind everywhere to an organised body of ecclesiastics is inevitable.[1]

Only let this great end be secured, and then, as Dr. Pusey has told us, 'there is no insurmountable obstacle to the union of the Roman, Greek, and Anglican communions.' A submissive return to the authority of the Church thus becomes our only chance of safety. 'Dissent,' it is thought, would, under such circumstances, 'undoubtedly break in pieces beneath the silent action of universal attraction;' or, *which is far more probable*, be broken up by the hammer of power.

Let us look these matters fairly in the face. The fundamental principle underlying all that agitates us in the present day is, a claim, common alike to Roman and Anglican, to an uninterrupted succession of the apostolate; to a teaching authority, akin to that of the apostles, exercised in interpreting the doctrine of Jesus Christ; to the exclusive right of administering what are called sacraments. Truly has it been insisted that when the Church of England yields this, she yields all. For, 'with a theory that so closely approximates to that of Catholic orthodoxy; with a liturgy drawn exclusively from Catholic sources; and with a catechism capable of imbuing the minds of her children with the most Catholic apprehension of the two principal sacraments—Bap-

[1] See Appendix. Note D. 'Church Authority.'

tism and the Holy Eucharist—who can doubt the ultimate reunion of the Anglican Church with the rest of Christendom?' Our choice, then, as we have been recently told, lies (and lies only) 'between a Christianity organised, hierarchical, and dogmatic,' and that simple dependence upon God alone, which, instead of producing—as some pretend it does—'a sinful uncertainty of mind,' really brings with it peace and joy in believing, and a true rest in the Holy Ghost.

That *extreme* views on the inspiration of Scripture, whether called plenary or verbal, when fearlessly and logically carried out, invariably strengthen the hands of the enemy is but too clear. They inevitably vest the final decision as to what the Book says *in man*; its value, therefore, is necessarily dependent on the existence and authority of an organised body called the Church.

It may indeed be said, and truthfully, that among the advocates of verbal inspiration and an infallible book, may be found a multitude who expressly repudiate Church authority. Those who do so, however, commonly fall back upon what in reality amounts to the same thing—the unquestioning acceptance, and, where it is possible, *the enforcement* of an hereditary or traditional theology, sometimes expressed in catechisms or other official documents, and sometimes in the more stringent form of public opinion, controlling the sect to which a man belongs. Such are the mischiefs which inevitably spring from modern pharisaism, and its idolatry of the Bible.[1]

On the other hand, supposing all that has been ad-

[1] See Appendix. Note E. 'The Idolatry of the Bible.'

vanced to be true, and that the distinction drawn between the historical and the ethical portions of the Bible is a just one—that *some* things, therefore, in Scripture are not properly God-breathed communications—*what have we lost?* By how much are we the poorer? What consolations have fled? What pillar has been withdrawn from the great spiritual edifice? To what extent, and in what way, is the Bible *less* to us than it was before? Surely it is hard to see that anything whatever has even been impaired in worth.

But it may be replied, '*What have we gained?*' Nothing, assuredly, in the way of compromise with the unbeliever. Nothing which, in itself, is likely to render either Christ or his Gospel less distasteful than it has always been to the worldly and the profane. Something, however, can scarcely fail to have been accomplished towards strengthening the faith of a class who have had their confidence in Divine truth shaken by assertions which will not bear close examination. Something, it may be hoped, towards satisfying such persons that instructed Christians do not believe that the Bible can be explained away, or that criticism can, step by step, undermine its revelations. Something, it may perhaps be added, towards the comfort of hope in souls that have stumbled at the word, *not* because of disobedience, but because under that name they have confused the human with the Divine. Something, therefore, towards the removal of perplexities from minds that have dwelt with a morbid interest on difficulties for which revelation is not responsible, and which, if incapable of being altogether removed may, at least, be so diminished as to lose their importance, and cease to have mischievous effects.

CHAPTER XI.

A POSTSCRIPT.

Two or three objections relative to matters discussed in the foregoing pages having been made in the various conversations which the author has had with intelligent doubters and others, he refers to them here in order that they may be taken for what they are worth. The first has been put thus:—

'You seem to think that the sceptic, while denying the authority of the Gospels, is inconsistent enough to give the evangelists credit for truly recording *what appeared to them* to be miraculous occurrences. This, however, is not the fact, since the unbeliever does not admit for a moment that the narratives were written down by eye-witnesses. Regarding the Gospels as having been penned at least half a century after the events they profess to record, he holds that the writers, whoever they might be, merely express *the opinions of the day* in which they wrote *respecting the facts*; that the narratives they give are not properly speaking *facts*, but the *interpretations* of a later age respecting the facts. He considers that a halo of wonder and supernaturalism *grew around* the history of Christianity in the early part of the first century, and that this was reflected in the writings of the evangelists. The dilemma, therefore, so often put, that these writers were either deceived or deceivers, he argues, falls to the ground. They need not, he says, have been either. The writers *necessarily* put upon the evangelic history the coloring of the traditional sources from which it was derived; they could not have done otherwise. How many times, he exclaims, in the world's history has a mass of supernatural belief *grown round* a nucleus of the purest religious idea! All religions are more or less cradled in such beliefs. Hence a man may deny the supernatural in the Bible and yet be a good Christian after all. Christianity is an all-embracing reality; it has actually moulded the whole civilisation of the modern world; it lives in society, speaks in our laws, and breathes more or less in the thoughts, feelings, and moral principles of every good man, whatever may be his speculative difficulties. Such an one cannot strip himself of Christianity if he would; and, therefore, whatever you may call him, he is a Christian, for his nature has been moulded by Christian influences.'

We reply: 'Belief in the miracles of our Lord and His disciples does not depend on the amount of evidence which can be brought forward in support either of the authorship of the Gospels or of the precise time when they were composed. Christianity itself, apart altogether from the particular narratives in question, rests on miracle. If Christ be not risen Christianity is a mere delusion. On the other hand, if the Redeemer *did* rise from the dead the supernatural is admitted.

To regard the statements of the evangelists—calm, unexcited, colorless as they confessedly are—as mere representations of the excited thoughts and feelings of a later age, tinged, or rather tainted, as in this case they must be, by the traditional sources from which they were derived, is, to say the very least of it, every way improbable, 'a most unlikely guess' at the best. Nothing, indeed, strikes one more than the comparatively little effect which, according to the narrative, the miracles appear to have produced *beyond* the limited circles in which they were performed. So abundant were they, so quietly were they wrought, so unpretending was the character of the worker, and so practically benevolent His end and aim, that they scarcely seem to have been regarded as wonders. The demand still was, 'give us a sign,' as if signs in abundance were not observable on every hand.

The fact that one great section of the Jews—the Pharisees—regarded the entire national history as miraculous, and lived and died in constant expectation of a supernatural deliverer; that another section—the Sadducees—denied the spiritual world altogether; and that a third—the Herodians—had become bound up with the support of things as they then were, far from being favourable to an easy credulity in relation to Christianity, must have wrought in an opposite direction. Those who believed that their 'own children' could miraculously cast out devils; Herod, who thought that John the Baptist had risen from the dead, and the many who considered Christ to be 'Elias, or one of the prophets' reappearing upon earth, were none of them men who, like modern sceptics, would deny the supernatural altogether. Rather would they, as believers in the possibility of miracles, look the more narrowly into the reality of those which were professedly wrought by Jesus and His apostles. That they did so, and found themselves unable to do more than attribute what they could not deny to the agency of Beelzebub, is evidence that the lapse of half a century was not needed in order to account for miraculous claims—that this element, however it may be regarded, was certainly *not an after-growth.*

Had there been in our Lord's time a prevailing disbelief in miracles, and half a century later a revived faith in them, there might be at least some plausible ground for supposing that this element gathered in the course of years around what was once only a religious idea. But there is no pretext for such a conclusion. Equally unreasonable is it to *assume* that no record was made of the facts by eye-witnesses, and at the time the events occurred; that side by side with a large body of persecuted believers, and with fixed institutions established as memorials of supposed facts, nothing should exist relating thereto beyond dim, hazy, and untrustworthy traditions.

The absurdity of the notion that every man is a Christian whose nature has, in spite of himself, been moulded by Christian influences, whatever may be the amount of his unbelief, is obvious, since on this showing, any virtuous Jew or heathen, who, from whatever circumstance, has come under the soul-elevating power of the ethical element in the New Testament, has a claim to be embraced in the Christian fellowship, which, if faith in the Redeemer be anything at all, is simply an extravagance.

The *second* objection taken is of a directly opposite character, and may be expressed thus:—

'It is not safe to allow that any sceptic can, in a true sense, be religious. No man can, properly speaking, be such who rejects the basis on which all practical virtue rests. No one can be good, so long as the root from which his supposed goodness springs is itself but rottenness.'

To this sweeping refusal to allow any quarter to the doubter, it may be replied that we have no right to reject the testimony of Christian men who know such persons well, and testify of some, at least, that their lives are pure, their spirit unworldly, and their scepticism reluctant. We have no right to assume that these men reject Christ, or that the root from which their virtues spring *is* rottenness. How much truth may be doubted, or even denied, without spiritual death, it is in many cases impossible for us to say; but we are surely justified in believing that where men, though 'perplext in faith, are pure in deeds,' where reverence for Scripture has not been cast off, where difficulties relate not so much to revealed facts as to human deductions intermingled therewith, there is good reason for cherishing hopes which, at least, forbid us to denounce without discrimination.

It must, however, be admitted that the union of principles which are pre-eminently Christian with the absolute rejection of Christ, is a feature peculiar to the unbelief of the present day, and that it is one which carries with it no common danger. The recent appearance of a volume of essays, written by Englishmen of high talent and standing, 'avowedly for the purpose of advocating certain views derived from the writings of M. Comte,' is indeed a sign of the times, since Comte not only held that the Roman Catholic system was the only genuine form of Christianity, but proposes to 'organise the education of the West by means of a body or order, which can only rest as its prototype, the Catholic system did, on a community of faith.'[1]

'The writers of the Essays generally regard Christian influences as pernicious, and there is hardly an essay in the volume which is free from attacks upon it; in some of the essays they abound, and are supported by misrepresentations of Christian teaching. Everywhere the quiet assumption is made that Christianity is a thing of the past, doomed, and rapidly passing away. Protestantism M. Comte never spoke of but with a protest as against a shapeless anarchical system, and he talks of being preserved from it with an unction worthy of a Romish zealot.' And yet the book contains very much that is good. The motto taken as the guide of all

[1] The Essayists are Richard Congreve, M. A., late Fellow and Tutor of Wadham College, Oxford; Frederick Harrison, M. A., Fellow and late Tutor of Wadham College, Oxford; E. S. Beesly, M. A., of Wadham College, Oxford, Professor of History at University College, London; E. H. Pember, M. A., late Student of Christ Church, Oxford; J. H. Bridges, M. B., late Fellow of Oriel College, Oxford; Charles A. Cookson, B. A., of Oriel College, Oxford; and Henry Dix Hutton, of Lincoln's Inn, Barrister-at-Law. In the paragraphs inserted referring to the work, it has been thought better to adopt the account given of it by the Rev. W. H. Fremantle, M. A., in the Cotemp. Rev. (xii.) than to offer any anonymous criticism. Mr. Fremantle's name and position furnish an adequate guarantee for the truthfulness of his statements. The title of the book is 'International Policy: Essays on the Foreign Relations of England.' Chapman and Hall.

moral and political speculation is one which every true Christian echoes from the bottom of his heart—'Vivre pour autrui.'

'The constant reference is to a certain ultimate state of human society which is believed to be approaching, and of which the secret, though not explained, is supposed to be with the writers.' Into any details relating thereto, so far as they can be gathered, it is *here* impossible to enter; but there is to be 'a high priest of humanity, who will be, more truly than any mediæval pope, the only real head of the Western world;' there are to be prayers, and priests, and sacraments, and by these the whole world is to be regenerated. 'Once,' it is said, 'let the reorganisation of the West be fairly secure, and a noble proselytism will become the principal collective occupation of the positive priesthood.'

A wild dream this must of necessity appear to every sensible man, and yet, if M. Comte's notions were mere hypotheses, liable to all manner of changes by his followers, why should we be constantly reminded, in a solemn manner, that we are in a state of transition, and that some final state, which M. Comte's disciples know of, is at hand to supersede the present 'transitional state, or state anarchy,' by which terms the present condition of Europe is constantly denoted?

[1] 'The system of this book, (International Policy), says Mr. Harrison in the second essay (p. 152), 'has already been stated in earlier pages (Mr. Congreve's Essay, pp. 36 and 41); *it implies the organisation of the West*, upon a system of common moral and intellectual principles, and on one uniform tone of public and private life; the whole animated and knit together by a common education and a common body of intellectual teachers and guides. How far we are from the realisation of this, it is not the part of this work to consider.'

Nor should it be unnoticed—although the authors of the volume are probably quite unaware of the fact—that writers on prophecy have, for the last thirty years, amid no little scorn, been repeating their conviction that the advent of some organisation of the kind anticipated is shadowed forth in the Apocalypse, and there associated with bitter and bloody persecution, under the headship of the last form of Antichrist.

Such, then, is one phase, and by no means an unimportant one, of the unbelief of the present day. Christianity scorned, and its missions derided, yet selfishness condemned, duty made supreme, the whole of Western Europe looked upon as one great commonwealth, with common sympathies and objects, each nation desirous of the good of the whole, rather than of its own, and all combining to spread their common civilisation among the other races of mankind.

With one thing it is impossible to help being struck, viz., the singular change that has taken place in the relative positions of Christianity and its opposite since Robert Hall published his celebrated sermon on 'Modern Infidelity.' *Then* scepticism was described as 'essentially and infallibly a system of enervation, turpitude, and vice,' leading to 'the frequent perpetration of great crimes, and the total absence of great virtues.' *Now*, the clergy are warned by this same school that 'no religious organisation can long hold its ground in popular esteem when confronted by a loftier morality than its own.' *Then* it was said of unbelief, 'attention to self is the spring of every movement and the motive to which every action is referred.' *Now* the motto taken as a guide by them is 'Vivre pour autrui,' and the principle kept continually in view, 'The subordination of politics to morals.'

Then priests of all kinds, *simply as such*, were hated. *Now* an order so called is regarded as essential to the regeneration of the world. *Then* Rome and unbelief appeared to have little or nothing in common. *Now*, whether consciously or unconsciously, they habitually support and strengthen each other. *Then* unbelievers alleged it to be a grievous defect in the morality of the Gospel, that it neglected to inculcate patriotism, and the Christian advocate had to urge that it was wise in God 'to decline the express inculcation of a principle so liable to degenerate into excess.' *Now* we are told our great object should be 'to bring into political relations the spirit of unselfishness,' and to regard love of country as a great evil when it conflicts with the love of the human race.

And yet, in spite of all these differences, the old hatred to Christianity prevails, and greatly should we err if we concluded that any essential change had actually taken place. It still remains certain that 'whenever the religious feeling or instinct in man works freely, without an historical revelation, it must beget a system of priestcraft; an intellectual priesthood it may be, but inevitably one more intolerant, exclusive, and oppressive than any other with which the world has ever been cursed.'[1]

The *third* objection, different from either of the preceding, will, it is to be feared, be a popular one. It runs thus:—

'Why meddle at all with this difficult and dangerous

[1] See Maurice's Lectures on the Religions of the World.

subject? True Christians, resting in implicit faith on Scripture, can only be unsettled and injured by learning that there is even room for a doubt regarding the absolute inspiration of any portion of the Bible. If there is indeed a weak point in the arguments usually brought forward to support either the plenary or verbal theory, far better is it to throw a cloak over such a defect than to unveil it before the world, however good may be the intention. Belief in what the Bible contains is necessarily to most persons a prejudice, and the cases are few in which this can be exchanged for a conviction. Why then shake a prejudice which is so useful when you are unable to ensure its being superseded by anything better?

'To the sceptic you can do no good. *His* mind is made up to reject a revelation which, if true, condemns him. He will only argue from your admissions that if it is lawful to draw any line between the inspired and uninspired in Scripture, the whole question of its acceptance or rejection comes to be one of *degree* only. The same criticism which you think justifies doubt in relation to the narrative of the execution of Saul's seven sons, carries him somewhat further, and if he ends in excluding the story of the Resurrection itself, he has only to thank you for the example.'

We reply: The ground here taken *assumes* that it is better for men to abide in error, if it can be made useful, than to arrive at truth if accompanied by possible danger. It is the old distrust of *the merely true* as such, and so far indicates want of confidence in Him who is emphatically 'the Truth.' Such is essentially the spirit of Rome, for it proceeds on the supposition that men must, at all hazards, be led into what may be regarded as the right path, whatever may be the means used. The end sanctifies all. This course is an immoral one, and cannot therefore be sustained. An unshaken faith in God, in truth, and in uprightness can alone deliver us from the wretched delusion involved in all such miserable expedients.

That any true Christian is likely to have his confidence shaken by honest investigation is not to be believed for a moment by anyone who really considers what Divine trust is, and the grounds on which it rests, That the hardened sceptic may be incapable of estimating the force of any reasoning which is presented to him in favour of the authority of the Bible is likely enough. But let us remember that the man thus spoken of was not always unimpressible. There was, in all probability, a time in his mental history, as there has been in that of most of us, when the syren voice of the doubter was listened to with a strange admixture of fear and wonder; when its charm was found rather in the feeling of independence that it flattered than in the force of its suggestions; when a bold treatment would have been successful; when an opposite course—timidity, distrust denunciation—on the part of the believer proved fatal. It is for men in this stage—and at the present moment they are a countless multitude—that we now write. Should they reflect on that which has been written it may surely be expected that to some the Book will be found beneficial, a hope which we would on no account exchange for the plaudits of a world, however 'religious' that 'world' might call itself.

As for the pretence—for it is really nothing better—

that to give up *anything* in the Bible is in effect to give up all; that if a line is to be drawn *anywhere* its place must be fixed by the caprice of the reader; it is enough to observe that the real question is *not* how much or how little may be regarded as human in Scripture, but *on what ground* the distinction in question is proposed to be made. Reason, it is granted, is not in itself adequate to judge as to what is or is not worthy of God. Taste, caprice, preconceptions of any kind have nothing whatever to do with the matter. If the rebuke to Balaam or the deliverance of Jonah are to be rejected because it seems incredible or grotesque that an ass should speak or a whale disgorge its living burden, we adopt a principle which certainly leads to the *construction* rather than to the reception of a Divine revelation. But if, on the contrary, we confine ourselves to the test of congruity; if we accept or reject *only on the ground* of the harmony or want of harmony which a statement has with other revelations, with all that God has taught us whether by the servant or by the Son regarding His own character and will; if we do this in dependence on the teaching of that Spirit which, as an unction from the Holy One, is given to 'the lowly heart and pure;' if we but follow the example of those early Christians who tried the spirits whether they were of God or not, we may be quite sure that the danger supposed is altogether imaginary, and that 'the honest mind, calmly seeking after God's truth in the spirit He approves, will not be at a loss to make sufficient distinction between religious or ethical truth and departments belonging to the natural and human.'

He who *wishes* to confound them will easily succeed

in doing so; but 'he who sincerely seeks to distinguish the minor parts, in which the correctness of inspiration does not necessarily lie, from the moral and religious elements constituting revelation proper,' may do so without difficulty. 'The religious and theological element,' says Dr. Pye Smith, 'or whatever contains religious truth, precept, or expectation, *cannot but appear perfectly distinct and manifest* to any man who understands language, and is not previously determined to pervert what is plainly before his eyes.'

One word more. Experience has taught us that, in the present day, the rejection of the Bible is almost invariably followed by painful questionings, sometimes as to the existence and sometimes as to the character of God. Let us realise the fact that it can scarcely ever be otherwise. Apart from Scripture, it is impossible to know anything of the Creator which can *assure* us either of His presence or His will; of His relation to us or of our condition before Him. How important, then, is it that the first beginnings of doubt should be *honestly* dealt with! How foolish to think or speak of the acceptance or rejection of 'the Book' as a light thing, so long as we come under the influences which Christianity has diffused over the globe. The truth or falsehood of the Bible, its worth or its worthlessness, is the great question of the day. It is not too much to affirm that the life or death of modern society hangs upon the issue.

NOTES.

A. (Chap. ii. p. 65.)

EMINENT WITNESSES.

The following, among others, may be quoted :—

Hooker. 'As incredible praises given unto men do often abate and impair the credit of their deserved commendation, so we must likewise take great heed, lest in attributing unto Scripture more than it can have, the incredibility of that do cause even those things which indeed it hath most abundantly to be less esteemed.' [1]

Baxter (Richard). 'Here I must tell you a great and needful truth, which ignorant Christians, fearing to confess, by overdoing tempt men to infidelity. The Scripture is like a man's body, where some parts are but for the preservation of the rest, and may be maimed without death. The sense is the soul of the Scripture, and the letters but the body or vehicle.' [2]

Tillotson (Archbishop). 'If any man is of opinion that Moses might write the history of those actions which he himself did, or was present at, without an immediate revelation of them; or that Solomon, by his natural and acquired wisdom, might speak those wise sayings which are in his Proverbs; or that the Evangelists might write what they heard and saw, or what they had good assurance of from others, as St. Luke tells us he did; or that St. Paul might write for his cloak and

[1] Hooker, p. 274. [2] Wordsworth's Christian Institutes.

parchment at Troas, and salute by name his friends and brethren; or that he might advise Timothy to drink a little wine, &c., without the immediate dictate of the Spirit of God: he seems to have reason on his side.'[1]

WARBURTON. 'Thus we see the advantages resulting from a PARTIAL INSPIRATION as here contended for and explained; it answers all the ends of a Scripture universally and organically inspired, by producing an unerring rule of faith and manners; and, besides, obviates all those objections to inspiration which arise from the too high notion of it, such as trifling errors in circumstances of small importance.'[2]

PALEY. 'The books (of the Old Testament) were universally read and received by the Jews of our Saviour's time. He and His apostles, in common with all other Jews, referred to them, alluded to them, used them: yet, except where he expressly ascribes a Divine authority to particular predictions, I do not know that we can strictly draw any conclusion from the books being so used and applied, besides the proof which it unquestionably is, of their notoriety and reception at that time.'[3]

SCOTT (Thomas). 'By the Divine inspiration of the Holy Scriptures, I mean such an immediate and complete discovery by the Holy Spirit to the minds of the sacred penmen of those things *which could not have been otherwise known*, and such an effectual superintending as to those things which they might be informed of by other means, as entirely to preserve them from error *in every particular which could in the least degree affect any of the doctrines or commandments* contained.'[4]

WATSON (Bishop). 'As to the apostles themselves, whenever they *wrote or spoke concerning Christianity* that fund of inspiration kept them right. But they were reasonable creatures as well as inspired apostles, and therefore could speak or write about common affairs as men that have the use of their reason without any inspiration can easily do.'[5]

[1] Sermon 168, p. 449, fol.
[2] Works, 4to, 1778, pp. 556, 557.
[3] Evidences of Christianity, p. 291.
[4] Essays, p. 3.
[5] Tracts, p. 446.

Tomline (Bishop). 'They (the sacred penmen) were sometimes left to the common use of their faculties, and did not upon every occasion stand in need of supernatural communication; but whenever and as far as the Divine assistance was necessary it was always afforded.'[1]

Whately (Archbishop). 'In the first place we should bear in mind what parts of the Bible are to be regarded as strictly and properly bearing the character of revelation. A great part of it is historical; and though we believe the sacred historians to have been under the guidance of the Holy Spirit to lead them *into all necessary religious truth*, to guard them against any material error, and in some few cases, to inform them of what could not be known by human means; yet, the very nature of history is such that it would be unreasonable to expect to find each single event that is narrated to be a matter of high importance.'[2]

Hinds (Bishop). 'To Religious instruction of whatever kind is confined the Scriptural character of Scripture, *the agency of the* Holy Spirit. It is not, therefore, truth of all kinds that the Bible was inspired to teach, but only such truth as tends to religious edification; and the Bible is consequently infallible as regards this, and this alone.'[3]

Smith (Dr. Pye). 'I regard as inspired Scripture all that refers to *holy things*, all that can bear the character of "Oracles of God," and admit the rest as appendages of the nature of private memoirs or public records, useful to the antiquary and the philologist, but which belong not to the rule of faith or the directory of practice. To this extent, and this only, can I regard the sanction of the New Testament as given to the inspiration of the Old. Inspiration belongs to Religious objects, and to attach it to other things is to lose sight of its nature, and misapply its design.'

'I can find no end of my anxiety, no rest for my faith, no satisfaction for my understanding, till I embrace the senti-

[1] Theology, pp. 21–2. [2] Essays, p. 223.
[3] On the Inspiration of Scripture.

ment that the qualities of sanctity and inspiration belong only to the religious and theoretical element which is *diffused through* the Old Testament; and that where this element is absent—where there is nothing adapted to communicate "doctrine, reproof, correction, or instruction in righteousness," nothing fitted to "make the man of God perfect, thoroughly furnished unto every good work"—*there* we are not called to acknowledge any inspiration, *nor warranted to assume it.*'[1]

Nine of these extracts are made from the 'Defence of the Rev. Rowland Williams, D. D., in the Arches Court of Canterbury, by James Fitzjames Stephen, M. A., of the Inner Temple, Barrister-at-Law, Recorder of Newark-on-Trent.' The three last are from 'The Text of the Old Testament Considered,' by Samuel Davidson, D. D.

B. (Chap. ix. p. 173.)

BIBLICAL INTERPRETATION.

A brief glance at the history of Biblical interpretation, regarded as a science, will alone be sufficient to explain how it is that the Sacred Volume has come to be regarded as indefinite in its teachings, and more or less unintelligible in its utterances. *Any book*, treated as it has been, must necessarily be stamped with that character.

The following sketch is abridged from an article on Interpretation, by Dr. Credner, found in Kitto's Biblical Cyclopædia, edited by Dr. W. L. Alexander of Edinburgh.

Three different modes of interpreting the Bible have at different periods been adopted: the GRAMMATICAL, the ALLEGORICAL, and the DOGMATICAL.

The *grammatical* mode of interpretation simply investi-

[1] Paper in Cong. Mag. (July, 1837), quoted from Davidson.

gates the sense contained in the words of the Bible. The *allegorical* maintains that the words of Scripture have, besides their simple sense, another which is concealed as behind a picture, and endeavours to find out this supposed figurative sense. The *dogmatical* endeavours to explain the Bible in harmony with the dogmas of the Church, following the principle of *analogia fidei.* The chief expedient adopted in order to effect *harmony* of interpretation has been to consider certain articles of faith to be LEADING DOCTRINES, and to regulate and define accordingly the sense of the Bible wherever it appeared doubtful and uncertain.

When the principle of one general Catholic Church was adopted, it was found difficult to select doctrines by the application of which to Biblical interpretation a perfect harmony could be effected. Yet *the wants of science* powerfully demanded a systematical arrangement of Biblical doctrines. This sense of need led first of all to allegorical interpretation. Origen argues thus: 'The Holy Scriptures inspired by God form an harmonious whole, perfect in itself, without any defects and contradictions, and containing nothing that is insignificant and superfluous. Grammatical interpretation leads to obstacles and objections which are inadmissible. Now, since the merely grammatical interpretation can neither remove nor overcome these objections, we must seek for an expedient beyond the boundaries of grammatical interpretation. The allegorical offers this expedient, and consequently is above the grammatical.'

Allegorical interpretation, however, it soon appeared, could not be reduced to settled rules, since it necessarily depends upon the greater or less influence of the imagination ; so in process of time there gradually sprung up the dogmatical mode, founded upon the interpretations of ecclesiastical teachers who were recognised as orthodox in the Catholic Church. This more and more supplanted the allegorical, which henceforward was left to the wit and ingenuity of a few individuals.

After the commencement of the fifth century, partly in consequence of the full development of the ecclesiastical system of doctrines defined in all their parts, and partly by continually increasing ignorance of the languages in which the Bible was written, interpretation was confined to the mere collection of explanations which had first been given by men whose ecclesiastical orthodoxy was regarded as unquestionable.

During the middle ages, however, allegorical interpretation prevailed, chiefly because it gave satisfaction to sentiment, and afforded occupation to free mental speculation.

When in the fifteenth century classical studies revived, grammatical interpretation, which, as a rule, goes hand in hand with progress, again rose to honour. It was especially by this weapon that the domineering Catholic Church was combated at the period of the Reformation; but as soon as the newly-sprung-up Protestant Church had been dogmatically established, it began to consider grammatical interpretation a dangerous adversary of its own dogmas, and opposed it as much as did the Roman Catholics themselves. Allegorical interpretation, therefore, in due time reappeared under the form of typical and mystical theology, as it always does when the dogmatic mode exercises an unnatural pressure.

Towards the beginning of the eighteenth century grammatical interpretation recovered its authority, and, in spite of continual attacks, towards the conclusion of that century it decidedly prevailed among German Protestants. During the last thirty years, however, both Protestants and Roman Catholics have again curtailed its rights and invaded its province, by promoting the opposing claims of dogmatical and mystical interpretation.

The question really demanding a settlement is this: Whether the rules and gifts which qualify a man for the right understanding of ordinary written language are, or are not, sufficient for rightly understanding the Bible? Most Biblical interpreters have declared such rules and gifts to be insufficient, because, say they, the Bible, having been written under the direct guidance of the Holy Ghost, is not to be measured by the common rules which are applicable only to the lower sphere of merely human thoughts and compositions. The result has been that interpretation has become neither more nor less than the art of understanding the Bible according to the particular ecclesiastical system that may be in vogue at any given period.

But surely it will be allowed that if God has deemed it desirable to reveal His Will to mankind by means of intelligible books, He must have intended that the contents of those books should be discovered in accordance with those general laws which are conducive to the right understanding of documents in general. For if this were not the case, He would have chosen insufficient and even contradictory means inadequate to the purpose He had in view, which cannot be supposed.

The interpretation which, in spite of all ecclesiastical opposition, ought to be adopted as the only true one, is unquestionably that which has in modern times been styled the Historico-Grammatical. This appellation has been chosen because the epithet grammatical seems to be too narrow and too much restricted to the mere verbal sense. It might be more correct to style it simply the Historical interpretation, since the word historical comprehends everything that is requisite to be known about the language, the turn of mind, and the individuality of an author, so far as this knowledge is needful in order rightly to understand his book.

C. (Chap. ix. p. 182.)

NATIONAL ESTABLISHMENTS.

Those—and they are possibly but few of the present generation—who have carefully read Coleridge's remarkable book 'On the Constitution of the Church and State according to the idea of each,'[1] will be aware that the author attaches, and not without reason, great importance to the distinction therein drawn between the National Church and the Church of Christ.

'The *Christian* Church,' he says, 'is a public and visible community, having ministers of its own, whom the State can neither constitute nor degrade, and whose maintenance among Christians is as secure as the command of Christ can make it: for "so hath the Lord ordained that they which preach the Gospel should live of the Gospel" (1 Cor. ix. 14). . . . 'It (the Church of Christ) is the opposite to the world only, asking of any particular State neither wages nor dignities, but demanding protection, that is, to be let alone.'

'The *National* Church is a public and visible community, having ministers whom the nation, through the agency of a constitution, hath created trustees of a reserved national fund, upon fixed terms and with defined duties, and whom, in case of breach of these terms or dereliction of those duties, the nation, through the same agency, may discharge.'

This distinction, although not formally drawn, is clearly involved in the conflicting definitions given of 'the Church' in the nineteenth Article of the Anglican communion, and in the work of its great defender, 'the judicious Hooker.'

According to the Article (xix.), 'The Church is a congregation of *faithful* men.' According to Hooker it is a mixed community of *faithful and unfaithful*, comprehending the worst as well as the best. 'It is known,' he says, 'by an external profession of Christianity, *without regard in any respect had* to the moral virtues or spiritual graces of any member of that

[1] 3rd Ed. Edited by Henry Nelson Coleridge, Esq. Pickering, 1839. This little work—'the only work,' says the editor, 'that I know or have ever heard mentioned that even attempts a solution of the difficulty in which an ingenious enemy of the Church of England may easily involve most of its modern defenders—Mr. Coleridge prized highly. The saving distinctions,' he said, 'are plainly stated in it, and I am sure nothing is wanted to make them *tell*, but that some kind friend should steal them from their obscure hiding-place, and just tumble them down before the public *as his own*.' (Table Talk, p. 5.)

body. Yea, although they may be impious idolators, wicked heretics, imps and limbs of Satan.' The apparent contradiction arises from the word 'Church' being used in totally different senses. By 'the Church' the framer of the Article evidently means *the Episcopal communion.* By the same phrase Hooker as clearly understands *the nation at large.*

Why, then, should these two distinct institutions, the Episcopal Church and the Church of the nation, always be dealt with as if they were one and identical? Why should the State not be able to exercise its right of legislating for the Church of the nation without at the same time interfering with the Christian liberty of the congregation of the faithful? The answer is obvious: Simply because these two having been once one, we continue, in defiance of facts, to act on the theory that the Episcopal Church is still the Church of the nation. We do so partly, no doubt, from the difficulty of perceiving how, in case of separation, the ministers of the nation could, if they wished it, be also ministers of the Episcopal communion; partly from the unwillingness of the clerical body, in spite of unfavourable statistics, to consent, *even for liberty*, to be regarded as anything less than the National Church.

To what extent these obstacles are capable of being overcome it is at present impossible to say; but the fact that, on the one hand, hostile seceders, embracing at least *half* of those who attend public worship at all, largely clamour for a change; that, on the other, demands hitherto unknown are now made by multitudes of the Established Clergy to Romanise the National Church at will; that a growing sense of the right of every Christian communion to regulate its own doctrine and discipline is pervading society; and yet that the English people, Protestant to the core, are as much as ever attached to their ancestral form of worship: these things combined will probably before long compel the enquiry whether or no it is not possible so to separate the Episcopal Church from the Church of the nation (or, as it should rather be expressed, from the *National Religious Institute*, for such would not properly speaking be a Church) that the one, whether ritualistic or otherwise, might enjoy all the liberty of a voluntary society, and the other be made acceptable to the multitudes who now reject and despise it.

This is not the place to discuss details. But it may not be amiss to say that the supposed difficulty of accomplishing such a change is probably exaggerated. The basis on which the separation in question might be effected is in some particulars obvious enough. The Apostles' Creed, and such portions of the Book of Common Prayer as are in harmony therewith, would remain in use, while the Nicene and Athanasian Creeds, the Offices, and the Communion Service would be appropriated by the Episcopal Church. Baptisms, marriages, and funerals, as more or less civil acts, might continue to be performed with suitable offices by the national clerisy, those who were dissatisfied with what they would regard as 'maimed rites' supplementing them by such additional services as they might deem necessary. The recognition of Dissenting baptisms, the presence of the Registrar in a Nonconformist place of worship in order to legalise a marriage, and quarrels about the right of sepulture in parochial churchyards would then all be rendered needless. That which is national would be treated nationally, while that which properly belongs to Churches would be left untouched by the State.

Parochial edifices would of course remain as public property in the hands of the respective parishes to which they already belong. The chapels-of-ease, the district churches, and all private endowments would properly fall into the hands of the Episcopal Church. Parochial organisation would be untouched. In every parish throughout the kingdom there would still remain the 'germ of civilisation,' and in the 'remotest villages a *nucleus* round which the capabilities of the place might crystallise and brighten.'

It is of course easy to multiply objections to any such

scheme, and especially on the ground that it would practically be found impossible so to recast the National Church as to make either its teaching or its offices acceptable to everybody. But this need not be attempted. The reconstruction would of course proceed on recognised facts, such as that England is a Protestant nation; that her laws and institutions are all based on Christianity as revealed in the Bible; that, as a fact, all but a very small number indeed of those who care about religion at all *agree* in great leading principles and doctrines.

That under any arrangement some clergymen would, as now, attach more importance to one class of religious thought than another; that some would be Broad and others Evangelical; that there would still be room for forbearance with one another can scarcely be doubted; but *essentially* no difficulties would arise at all corresponding in importance to those which now trouble us. We should at least be delivered from the inconsistency of attempting by Parliamentary authority to change or to modify the formularies of a Church which, if a Church at all, may well resist all pressure on the part of the State to force its doctrine. The appointment of a clergyman, whether vested as now in patrons or given to the parish, might easily be ordered, and his removal, if needful, would be under the jurisdiction of the courts of law.

Perhaps it is not too much to say that if the distinction here urged had originally been recognised, the long struggle of Puritanism for liberty of conscience would have been rendered needless, and Dissent at the present day might have been unknown. Supplementary fellowships of a voluntary character would have supplied all deficiencies, and the Church, instead of being the deadly antagonist of a multitude of sects, would have been the fruitful mother of as many independent communities as the necessities of the case, whether arising from spiritual needs or from changes of opinion, might in course of time have required.

The error of the Reformers, or rather of those who yielded

to their influence, was that they failed to see, or seeing disregarded, the fact that the great ecclesiastical system from which they had broken off was at once a polity and a religion; that if in one aspect it was *a power* having its centre at Rome, in another it was *a conviction* having its root in the individual conscience. Had they regarded this aright they would, as statesmen, have dealt with Romanism somewhat differently. Religion, as such, under whatever form, would have been let alone. It would then have been perceived that Protestantism, from its very nature, must necessarily increase *individuality of belief*; and suitable provision having been made for the development of this inevitable tendency, by absolute freedom being secured to each and all to supplement what they felt to be wanting by voluntary action, an institution would have sprung into existence which would have proved, far more than any national *Church* ever has or can do, a true bond of unity; at once loyal to the monarch and acceptable to the people.

This result would have followed, simply because a provision for social worship and public teaching, the want of men in general, would in that case have been fully met. God would have been recognised nationally without individual consciences being interfered with; and everything pertaining to the peculiar religious convictions of each separate person—to his personal relations to God and duty, would have been left to be met by that voluntary provision which men are always willing to make when the religious instinct has been thoroughly awakened, and earnestness has taken the place of indifference. Need it be observed that to a national clerisy chosen and controlled as these would be, separated from any particular Church, and therefore without a motive to proselytism, the superintendence of the education of the nation might well be entrusted.

To speak of embracing Wesleyans and other seceders in the Church of England, by absorbing them, after they have built so many thousands of places of worship, and when, by means thereof, they can secure good incomes for their ministers, is the most idle of dreams. A Protestant Church in a free country like our own can never successfully imitate the Church of Rome by uniting to herself different orders under *control* of any kind. But she can do what is far better. She can take under her wing all forms of devout thought. She can win them to herself by the love of a large heart, and by the willing recognition, nay the honouring, of an individuality which is the offspring of freedom, the proof of earnestness, and the stability of all that is true and good.

The great error of the Church of England, regarded as a national establishment, has been that she has never had faith in herself; she has never had strength to believe in anything better than mere *outward* conformity or professed unity of opinion. But it cannot be the true policy of any national Church thus to necessitate if not to promote secession. On the contrary, her voice should always be, 'Obey conscience, follow truth, but, if possible, abide with your brethren. We may not be one in all points, but we can at least unite in common prayer and praise, and in a common recognition of the Giver of every good and perfect gift.'

England swarms with Dissenters only because the Church of England has never allowed any safety-valve for Christian zeal or individual convictions. She may yet make herself the Church of the nation if she will, but it must be by separating herself as an establishment alike from the Episcopal and from every other Church. How long that opportunity may last none can say. In Ireland the time for so doing has perhaps already past. Nothing in all probability will satisfy a people whose public sentiment is formed by a priesthood ever panting after pre-eminence, but *possession* of the revenues of the Church, or, if this cannot be had, their secularisation. Yet who does not feel that, *if it were possible* to devote these funds to any religious service which could be accepted, *as far as it went*, by Romanists as well as Protestants, how much better such a disposal of them would be than to employ them in endowing rival Churches or in any work of a merely secular character.

Those who may be disposed to meet these observations with sarcasm or scorn, may well be reminded that the *root-thought* on which they have proceeded belongs to a man who is universally admitted to have been one of the deepest thinkers of his age; a man who was Conservative in his politics, and more than usually attached to the Episcopal Church. Nor should the hints he has offered be regarded as unworthy of consideration because intended to be worked out by others whenever a time should arrive in which they would be listened to.

D. (Chap. x. p. 195.)

CHURCH AUTHORITY.

The position and claim of the Church as a great teacher, and as a guide to truth, cannot be separated from any fair enquiry into the place which Scripture ought to occupy in the formation of our beliefs. The existence or non-existence of an institution claiming the right sometimes of deciding *what is* truth, and sometimes of supplementing that truth by tradition, cannot but be an important element in all investigations bearing upon the Bible.

Nor is the point at issue, as is generally supposed, merely one *of degree*. The thing needing to be established is, not to what extent any existing ecclesiastical body may or may not have authority in controversies of faith; nor yet, whether or no, any actual Church holds in its own bosom a deposit of apostolic tradition; but whether any such body, having Divine authority for its institution, *exists in the world*. For if it does, nothing can be more obvious than that to its decisions, so far as it is empowered to give them, it becomes all of us to bow.

Hitherto this great question has been treated rather with reference *to the extent* of power claimed by any given Church, than to the reality or non-reality of the existence of such an organisation by Divine appointment. That authority of *some kind* or other over opinions, as well as over conduct, is vested in all Churches, however small or sectarian they may be, seems everywhere to be taken for granted.

Of course, so long as it is understood that this claim merely implies that, like secular associations, religious bodies may justly fix the conditions on which any person shall be received into, or retained in, their fellowship, no one has a right to dispute its propriety. But more than this is commonly meant; since all alike imagine they have the Divine sanction for what they do, and act accordingly. Leaders of sects may not indeed ask to be regarded as successors of the apostles; they may, on the contrary, energetically disclaim all such assumptions; and yet they both may and do not unfrequently *exercise the power* such a succession is supposed to confer, with far more stringency than those who put forward higher pretensions.

The question needing to be settled is, whether or no Christ and His apostles ever appointed successors, or ever gifted any man or body of men with power or ability to decide for others what ought or ought not to be believed.

Put in this way, the enquiry primarily, if not exclusively, bears upon such ecclesiastical bodies as have formally demanded the recognition of their right to settle controversies, by virtue of a commission received from Christ.

The reasoning by which this claim has hitherto been sustained cannot but be regarded as in man yrespects very unsatisfactory. It is argued, that inasmuch as probably a quarter of a century must have passed away before any Gospel or Epistle was produced; that as those who at length did write tell us for the most part that they were moved to do so by passing circumstances; that as they had evidently no thought of leaving behind them any *full* confession of faith; that since they did not affirm *in detail* the doctrine of the Trinity, or expound other mysteries; and since there is no trace of a collection of apostolical writings, or of the formation of a New Testament canon by John or any other influential Christian of the apostolic age, it could never be intended that men should take the Scriptures *alone* as their rule of faith, or that they should seek *in them* exclusively for a knowledge of God's revelation.

This view is supposed to find confirmation in the fact that Paul bids Timothy commit to faithful men *what he had 'heard'* from apostolic lips, that they might teach others also, and that he commands both the Corinthians and the Thessalonians to hold fast '*the traditions*' they had been taught. These unwritten teachings, therefore, as handed down by the Church are, it is asserted, essential to the securing of Christian doctrine in all its fulness, pure and certain through all generations.

Further, it is argued, that as Christianity was but an outgrowth of Judaism, the ancient priesthood had to be replaced by the spiritual succession of duly-appointed instructors, and that as the first Christians had received apostolic teaching not as the word of man, but as the Word of God, a provision was needed for securing to after-times a like repose in authority by the appointment of a living, ever-speaking tribunal open and accessible to all.

Whether such authority is supposed to centre in an individual, as the Pope, or in a body like the Church, matters little. The Romanist of course holds to the former; and in so doing maintains that the first deposit of doctrine was intended to have an organic growth, and to expand from its roots by a law of inward necessity, and in a manner corresponding to the intellectual needs of believers in different ages. There was to be, he says, a constant building up of doctrine as a progressive development, a mapping out of its details, and an exhibition of its full contents, secured and fixed by ecclesiastical decision, and all was to be accomplished under the guidance of the Paraclete, the teacher given to the Church.

It is not needful to enquire how much of this is held only by Romanists, how much belongs to Anglicanism, or how much is involved in the action of every Nonconforming community. What we want to know is, whether the *root-idea* has, or has not, any good foundation; whether there is really any reason to believe that the provision spoken of was ever made. The words of St. Paul, whether to Timothy or to the Gentile churches, prove nothing, unless it can be shown that the traditions he refers to were distinct from, or additional to, what is now embodied in the Gospels and the Epistles. The entire question is one of fact, one therefore respecting which we can know nothing, beyond what is left on record in Scripture.

Now, *there* we find no trace of any teaching similar in character to that which is supposed to be so essential. The apostles do not merely tell people what they ought to believe, as if that were enough; they do not even ask that anything should be received, simply on their responsibility or authority. St. Paul utterly disclaims any wish to have dominion over the faith of his converts. 'By faith' he says, 'ye stand.' 'We are but helpers of your joy.' To the Corinthians he writes, 'I speak as unto wise men, judge ye what I say.' The Galatians he warns not only against men who might preach another Gospel, but against himself if he should ever be led to do so. St. Peter exhorts elders 'as also an elder.' St. John directly appeals to his hearers as able to distinguish between truth and falsehood. All the apostles, in short, seem to have regarded themselves chiefly as witnesses of facts. When a new one had to be chosen in place of Judas, the reason given is, that he might be a witness with the rest of the resurrection. Everything they teach, is presented in the simplest form possible. Nothing can be found at all corresponding to the scholastic definitions of later times; nothing tending to indicate that such definitions would ever be desirable.

The evangelical narrative, as we have it, leaves quite a contrary impression to that which assumes the formal appointment of a body of men as in any way inheritors of apostolic powers or apostolic wisdom. The few believers are gathered together in fellowships of the simplest character, that as 'sheep among wolves,' they may exhort and strengthen one another. Elders chosen from their midst are appointed over them, and endowed with gifts fitting them, in the absence of written documents, rightly to teach and govern these infant communities. They 'break bread' together in memory of their Lord, apparently without the intervention of any officer of the Church. They possess, but they have no power of communicating gifts, either of speech or healing. Even Philip, the signally-honoured evangelist, cannot confer any of these endowments on his converts. Everything indicates that with the last man on whom the last of the apostles laid hands all miraculous power in the Church ceased and determined, and with that power all apostolic authority. Henceforward, true Christians appear to be essentially on a level, alike members of that royal priesthood of which Christ was the great Head and High Priest, although differing in talent and in work. Not from Scripture, certainly, can it be shown that Christ or His apostles ever framed an organization in any respects corresponding to what we call THE CHURCH.

How, then, came such an institution into existence? For nothing can be plainer than that about a hundred years after the death of John, *it appears*, although in anything but apostolic garb. All is altered. 'No other change,' says Dean Stanley, 'equally momentous has ever since affected its fortunes; yet none has ever been so silent and secret. The Church has now become history, the history not of an isolated community or of isolated individuals, but of an organized society, incorporated with the political systems of the world.'

Was this change, then, healthy development—the fore-intended growth of the acorn into the oak? or was it corruption—the first signal indication of that new order of things which then so mysteriously manifested itself, at once as an evil and a good: good in so far as it reared saints and subdued Paganism in the Roman empire; evil in its later developments culminating in the Papacy? A satisfactory answer to this question would solve many difficulties.

Hard is it to believe that a Church which produced so many Christian heroes, so many great and good men, should, in any sense whatever, be worthily called a 'Mystery of Iniquity.' Harder still, however, is it to imagine, on a review of the superstitions encouraged and the persecutions carried on for ages by its ecclesiastical tribunals, literally drunk with the blood of the saints; its Christianity so dead and morally degraded that nothing but the inroads of an impostor like Mahomet could cleanse the plains of Asia of the impurities it had nurtured there; its only religion, a religion of sacraments, under the guise of which the pastors of the Church had, as Coleridge puts it, 'gradually changed the life and light of the Gospel into the very superstitions they were commissioned to disperse, and thus *paganized* Christianity in order to *christen* paganism.' Hard is it to see in such a Church anything but a profound mystery of God, a mystery of spiritual evil, a mystery of iniquity. Be this, however, as it may, nothing can certainly be deduced either from its past or its present existence, or from the past or present history of any of the Reformed Churches, which can for a moment sustain the assertion that God has committed the development of doctrine or the power of decision in cases of doubt to any body of men, however earnest or good they may be, or however much they may have accomplished in the spread of the Gospel, in the civilisation of nations, or in the regions of benevolent activity.

E. (Chap. x. p. 196.)

IDOLATRY OF THE BIBLE.

'Idolatry of the written Word expresseth itself in the holy—but I call it unholy—notion, which they have taken up concerning inspiration, that the very words are inspired, and the writers were but organs of voice for that Word. . . . And in the same spirit they require of you at once to believe *the Book* as the Word of God, by one act of faith to adopt it, then to read it and bow down before what you read. That is to make the Book an idol, and then prostrate your soul unto it. And by so doing, you shall make your soul a timorous creature of superstition, or a blind worshipper of sounds and sentences; but never a child of the Spirit of God. Such notions flow not from orthodox doctrine which saith unto every man, Read this Word with what persuasion of its Divine authority you presently have, and affect not more than you really have, for that is falsehood or superstition, which God abhorreth. Bring to it the faculties of mind which you presently have, and peruse it with the desire to be enlightened in the deep things which it containeth, and the Spirit will open your soul to understand it more and more, and dispose your heart to receive it more and more, and constrain your will to obey it more and more; and as your soul grows into its confirmation more and more, you will believe it more and more, and your faith in its inspiration will grow with your spiritual growth and strengthen with your spiritual strength.'—The Idolatry of the Bible, by the Rev. Edward Irving.

From an article on the Theology of Luther, by the Rev. Dr. Dorner, Contemporary Review, No. xii.

(1.) 'Holy Scripture, in its real message and purport, receives its full credentials to the heart, by the illumination of the Spirit kindling in us a Divine assurance of the truth of this message —an assurance infinitely superior to any mere reliance on the canon of the Church, and on the correctness of the Church's judgment with regard to Scripture.'

(2.) 'Scripture can only be understood by a kindred mind and spirit. That which is necessary to salvation is intelligible to all who are spiritually disposed, and inequalities in mental culture and philological skill are, in everything material, compensated by the *perspicuity* of the Scripture. The believer is the instrument which Scripture creates for itself by means of which to interpret itself.'

(3.) 'The expounder is not to expound Scripture after the standard of any human conception of its doctrine, be that standard the Apostles' Creed, the *regula* or *analogia fidei*, or the teaching of the Church. He who asserts such standard to be necessary, denies the perspicuity of Scripture. The only analogy for exposition is the principle that one scripture cannot contradict another.'

(4.) 'Luther makes no difficulty in allowing, that in externals, not only Stephen, but the sacred writers themselves have fallen into inaccuracies. The worth of the Old Testament is not diminished in his eyes by the concession that several of its pieces have been worked up by various hands. What matters it, he asks, with reference to the Pentateuch, if Moses did not write it?'

(5.) 'Luther recognises in Scripture not merely something Divine, but something human. The German Reformer unquestionably draws a distinction between the word of God and the Holy Scripture, not merely in the form, but also in the purport of the message.'

(6.) Luther 'awards to faith a right of judging the canon on grounds not arbitrary, but objective and dogmatic; and quite distinct from any investigations of the genuineness and antiquity of its parts. . . . The right of faith to judge and criticise Scripture is, however, a negative right, reducing itself to the denial of canonical authority, to all that would contradict faith. And as faith must agree with Scripture, *this judgment of Scripture by faith* reduces itself ultimately to *a judgment of Scripture by itself.* To the power of interpreting itself, which he ascribes to Scripture, corresponds in his system the power of Scripture to decide what is really Scripture. . . . . The process of combining faith with the word of God must be continuous; we must be always *reconciling Scripture and the Christian consciousness*, in order to obtain that full and undoubting certainty which consists in the union of the personal and subjective with the objective word of God in Scripture. Thus, the certainty and joy of faith is not suspended for Luther by allowing criticism all its rights; nor, on the other hand, does Scripture lose in value and authority by the emphasis he lays on faith, but rather gains in these respects, inasmuch as Scripture becomes an internal authority with which faith cannot dispense.

THE END.